MA ✔ KU-637-254 OLO

MALLORCA

with Local Tips

There are six symbols to help you find
your way around this guide:

for Marco Polo recommendations - the best in each category

for all the sites with a great view

for places frequented by the locals

where young people get together

(A1)
map references

follow this route for the best sights on the island

MARCO ⊕ POLO

Other travel guides and language guides in this series:

Amsterdam • Crete • Cyprus • Gran Canaria • Paris

French • German • Spanish

*Marco Polo would be very interested to hear your
comments and suggestions. Please write to:*

*World Leisure Marketing Ltd
Marco Polo Guides
9 Downing Road, West Meadows
Derby DE21 6HA England*

*Our authors have done their research very carefully, but should any errors or
omissions have occurred. the publisher cannot be held responsible for any injury,
damage or inconvenience suffered due to incorrect information in this guide.*

Cover photograph: Helga Lade/Assmann
*Photographs: Lade: BAV/Kreicihwost/Welch/Wrba/Simone/Morell (9, 17, 22, 32, 36, 54, 57, 82, 85);
Mauritius/Coll/Pigneter/Vidler/Mollenhauer/Bohnacker (4, 26, 28, 30, 31, 35, 60, 71),
Gierth (38, 78), Burgmer (45), Rawi (jacket flap, 11),
Susan (50), Vidler (12, 58, 63);
Touristik-Marketing GmbH (72)
Cartography: Mairs Geographischer Verlag, Hallwag*

*1st English edition 1996
© Mairs Geographischer Verlag, Ostfildern Germany
© International rights: Mairs Geographischer Verlag/Hachette
Author: Gabriela Kunze
English edition: Craig MacInnes, Cathy Muscat, Emma Kay
Editorial director: Ferdinand Ranft
Design and layout: Thienhaus/Wippermann
Printed in Italy*

CONTENTS

Discover Mallorca

Far from the madding crowd, Mallorca is full of surprises,
offering a wealth of holiday options

The word Mallorca conjures up a multitude of images, many of them, it has to be said, predominantly negative. Most people immediately associate the island with cheap package holidays, crowded beaches, half-built hotels, discos, plenty of booze, fish and chips and cups of tea on the beach. Not very exotic to say the least! Mallorca is regarded as one of the prime victims of mass tourism, but this impression is a very superficial one. If you take the time to look a little more closely, you will discover a completely different Mallorca. It is a beautiful island, with a perfect climate and a good standard of living, where it is possible to have a peaceful and memorable holiday as far from the noise, stress and hustle and bustle of modern life as you can possibly get.

The beaches in the Bay of Palma provide the classic picture of Mallorca as a package holiday island. It is a huge tourist enclave, with more than 250

Dramatic scenery from a traditional house perched on a cliff top

hotels dominating a 5-km stretch of coastline between the former fishing villages of S'Arenal and Can Pastilla. Statistics show that the Playa de Palma is invaded by tens of thousands of holiday-makers every day during the summer season, who then pour into the pubs, restaurants and discos around the hotels at nightfall. This is all that many visitors see, or indeed want to see, of the island, which is a real pity because a trip just a few hundred metres inland from this concrete jungle transports you into a completely different world.

Here, the first thing that strikes you is the silence – that still, peaceful calm that is so uncharacteristic of the 20th century. The air is filled with the scent of lemon, lavender and rosemary. The country roads twist and turn, running alongside the walls of extensive country estates, and the breathtaking mountains to the north and west are always visible. Here and there rugged stone farmhouses nestle in the landscape. The amazing thing is that although physically you're not that far from the built-up coastline, it really does feel as if you are a million miles away. It is precisely these contrasts which make Mallorca such a fascinating holiday destination.

Raucous noise and complete stillness are close neighbours on Mallorca. Llucmajor is an honest, unromantic and not particularly picturesque country town, which lies only 12 km inland from the main tourist resorts. The narrow peaceful streets remain pretty empty during the day, as the 20 000 or so inhabitants are either at home, in the factory or in the fields. An important centre for the shoe industry, Llucmajor is surrounded by rich agricultural land, where apricots and almonds are cultivated in the fertile soil. There are only a few places where you can spend the night here, as most of the hotels are concentrated along the coast.

Given that tourism provides 75% of the island's income, does this mean then that Arenal is more important than Llucmajor? The tourist industry more important than the cultivation of apricots? Well, whichever way you look at it, Mallorca without tourism would be a 'holy land in hellish poverty', a green paradise with a feudal system. Mallorca enjoys the highest per capita income in the whole of Spain thanks to tourism. But even though much of the natural beauty of the coastal areas has been destroyed through development, the greater part of the island remains relatively unspoilt. If you want to discover the real Mallorca, far from the 'madding crowd', you only have to venture a little way beyond the main resorts to find it.

In geological terms, Mallorca isn't all that old. It was only 15 million years ago that 3700 square kilometres of rock appeared in the Mediterranean as a result of pressure from the African continental plate. The location was a fortunate one – 39.5° north and 3° east – endowing the island with a mild and hospitable climate which, apart from more recently attracting the development of today's tourist market, also attracted a number of different conquerors and settlers over the centuries, all of whom have left their mark on the island and its people.

Part of this legacy can be found in the character of the Mallorcans today. The ability to make the best of things, to turn conquest and defeat to the best advantage, and the instinct for survival can all be explained by the fact that at some time or other Mallorca has seen all of history's great conquerers come and go – Phoenicians, Greeks, Romans, Arabs, Vandals, Vikings, Byzantines and Moorish pirates.

It is not only in the mental outlook of the islanders that this history can be felt, it also shows in their physical characteristics. Take a look at some of the locals in Palma and you can see traces of their ancestry – Roman soldier, Moorish scholar and classical Greek – in their looks and bearing. This is hardly surprising when you consider that after the Greeks left Mallorca, the period of Roman rule lasted for about 1000 years, from 123 BC to AD 903, before the Moors finally conquered the island.

The Romans brought olive trees and viticulture as well as

HISTORY AT A GLANCE

c. 2000 BC
Seafarers from the Eastern Mediterranean settle on the island.

c. 1000 BC
The first Phoenician trading posts are established.

c. 800 BC
The Greeks challenge Phoenician supremacy and attempt to bring Mallorca within their sphere of influence.

123 BC
The Romans take control of the island. They import olive trees, cultivate the first vineyards, found cities, build roads, bridges, theatres and strongholds. Latin becomes the main language.

End of 3rd Century AD
Conversion of entire island to Christianity completed.

AD 750
The first Arab and Viking raids.

903
Moors from Morocco conquer the island.

1229
Christian forces, under King Jaime I of Aragón, defeat the Moors.

1276
Jaime II, son of Jaime I, declares himself King of Mallorca.

1348
Plague wipes out a third of the island's population.

1349
After the defeat of Jaime III's army by the forces of King Pedro IV of Aragón in the battle of Llucmajor, Mallorca becomes a province of Aragón.

17th Century
Famine strikes: skilled workmen and peasants forced to emigrate.

18th Century
Resurgence of the island's fortunes under the Bourbon King, Charles III of Spain.

1905
The Mallorcan Tourist Association, the Fomento de Turismo, is founded.

1920-30
The Hotel Formentor is opened. Palma has more than 3000 hotel and guest beds. The first 'foreign colonies' are established.

1950
The first charter flight arrives.

1962
The airport handles more than a million passengers.

1983
The Balearic Islands achieve the status of an autonomous region, with the setting up of the 'Comunitat Autónoma de les Illes Balears'.

1994
The airport handles more than 12 million passengers.

Latin, from which the languages spoken on the island today evolved (see p. 14). The Romans also gave the island its first infrastructure, much of which is still in use today. They founded cities and set up market-places, built roads and bridges, developed agriculture and an economic system based on the long-term view. The Moors added to the infrastructure created by the Romans, using their knowledge of mathematics, medicine, astronomy and navigation, and contributing their own expertise in water supply and horticulture. They were the ones who determined much of the shape which the Mallorcan landscape still has today. They planted apricot, almond and peach orchards on the plains and lemon and orange groves on the mountain slopes, bequeathing a richly cultivated island to the Christian conquerors who supplanted them.

One thing that neither the Romans nor the Moors introduced to the island was the palm tree, which didn't actually appear until the initial tourist boom in the mid-19th century. Around this time, Mallorca became popular with artists and writers who came here to escape the 'modern' world. The palm trees were imported to line the newly laid-out promenades, designed for visitors and locals alike to stroll along.

Among the first celebrities to put Mallorca on the tourist map were George Sand, the writer, and her lover, Frédéric Chopin. They spent some time in the winter of 1838/39 in a gothic monastery in Valldemossa (see p.58). She subsequently described their 'romance in the rain'

in her book, *A Winter on Mallorca*. In 1897, the German Archduke Ludwig Salvator von Habsburg-Lothringen and Bourbon, who lived near Valldemossa on the north coast, published an extensive work of several volumes on the Balearic islands. This drew the attention of the German people to the island and further contributed to its renown. In 1911, the Catalan writer Santiago Rusiñol, a friend of the young Picasso, published his influential book *Mallorca - Isla de la Calma,* which became a bestseller and was translated into all the major European languages. Not long after this, Adam Diehl, an Argentinian entrepreneur, established the Hotel Formentor, situated in the picturesque bay of Cala Pí de la Posada, which attracted Europe's intellectual elite.

The Mallorcans were quick to catch on to the enormous economic potential of their beaches and development soon began on the 'great sands' of Arenal. Visitors came and liked what they saw and the word spread. In 1923, the beach at Arenal was still divided into three separate sections: one for men, one for women, and one for animals! It was English and American women who were the first to challenge this segregation, braving the stares (not all of them disapproving) of the men as they bathed from the same stretch of sand. Their example soon caught on and even the islanders themselves began to make use of their beaches during the hot summers. In 1950, the first British and German charter flights landed at Palma and in 1962, only 12 years later, the airport handled over one million

Cala Millor: Mallorca's second-largest holiday complex

passengers. Mass tourism had well and truly arrived!

There are some 179 beaches in all on Mallorca, ranging from wide sweeping stretches of sand to tiny secluded coves and bays. You can find both crowded beaches and empty beaches – the choice is yours. If you lined the beaches up end to end, you would get a stretch of sand about 50 km long – around a tenth of the island's coastline. If, as has been said, the tourist areas have tended to distort this landscape, then it's worth remembering that only about 30% of the island's coastline has really been affected, leaving the other 70% in its natural state.

This proportion is unlikely to change much in the future, thanks to the Coastal Protection Law, the *Ley des Costas,* introduced in 1988, which controls coastal development in the whole of Spain. Any new developments must be built at least 100 m away from the sea, and existing hotels, private villas and urban developments situated directly on the coast are prohibited from expanding. In some cases, demolition orders have actually been enforced.

The realization that the future of tourism depends on the environment and sensible development came fairly late in the day to Mallorca, but it did come, and the tourist authorities are doing all they can to ensure that visitors will want to return again and again to the island. This has led to a different approach to tourism in general – the emphasis is now more on 'quality tourism', rather than on cheap package tourism, with its 'quantity not quality' ethos. To this end the Balearic Ministry of Tourism has made funds available for renovation and restoration work on all hotels that are more than five years old. Any new hotels and apartment complexes must come up to four or five-star standard. This is the most determined attempt yet by the authorities to improve the existing hotels and to encourage the development of higher-quality accommodation on the island, something which Mallorca had sadly lacked for years. At the moment, there are only six hotels in the five-star category and around 60 of four-star standard. With their 24 000 beds, they represent about 8% of the 200 000 or so beds available on Mallorca.

Other ways in which the authorities are attempting to encourage more quality tourism is by building new golf courses and yachting marinas. They also promote 'permanent' tourism by advertising the island as 'Europe's holiday home'.

Mallorca differs from many exotic islands, where unimaginable wealth contrasts sharply with abject poverty, and the tourist gets a cheap holiday courtesy of cheap labour. The Mallorcan people have all reaped the financial benefits of tourism and demand the same standard of living and status symbols that those who visit their country enjoy. They are relatively well-off today and aim to keep it that way.

So when's the best time to go? Well, that depends entirely on what kind of holiday you're looking for. If you're looking for sun, sea and sand then you should go in June, July or August. If, on the other hand, you want to get to know a bit more about the island, then almost any month in the year would be ideal. The fact that Mallorca is nearer to the Equator than it is to the North Pole may explain the 3000 hours of annual sunshine, but it doesn't mean that the island is perpetually bathed in sunlight. However, even in the depths of winter, the temperature rarely drops below 10°C. The Serra del Nord, the mountain range that runs along the north coast, has some 40 peaks over 1000 m high which protect the rest of the island from the ravages of winter. The strong winds that often whistle down their slopes can also have an effect on the climate. There is an old saying on the island: 'Hasta el cuarenta de mayo no te quites el sayo', which means 'don't discard your coat until the 40th day of May' (i.e. 10 June). However, for tourists, summer can be said to begin at Whitsun, and high season, which used to start around the middle of July, now begins in the middle of June. With the rising temperatures come rising prices, and an increase in the number of tourists which reaches its peak in August. This is when Palma takes on the appearance of a ghost town – shops and offices close, chemists take turns to be open and workshops operate only part-time. The airport, however, is as hectic as ever, with a jet full of holiday makers landing and taking off every two minutes. Tour guides, bus and taxi drivers work till they drop, as do waiters, chambermaids, chefs and hotel managers. August can seem endless and the occasional thunderstorm doesn't do much to clear the atmosphere. Clouds conceal the mountain tops, while the plain bakes under the relentless sun.

September can also bring a few hot sticky days, but the signs that autumn is approaching are there - thunderstorms, heavy rain and torrential flooding. *Gota fría* is what the locals call the first cool drops of rain. Then comes an Indian summer when a period of pleasant, balmy weather sets in, usually lasting until well into October. Even the beginning of November can be quite hot and sunny, much to the delight of those desperate to get a tan for the winter. This is when you need two sets of clothing. If the sun is shining, it's still incredibly warm, especially between midday and three in the afternoon, but in the morning and evening the air can turn chilly. In early December a small miracle happens – the *calmas* or *el pequeño verano*, little summer – which brings clear, mild days, and only the hint of a breeze. At this time of year, the crisp blue sky, the fresh green countryside and the bright yellow sun make for a striking landscape, evocative of a Miró painting. This is the best time of year to see Palma Cathedral, as the light is most flattering in the winter months. It can snow in January and February, but the first signs of Spring are also seen in these early months with the blossom from the millions of almond trees. They start to flower in the east near Portocristo and by the end of February a blanket of colour has spread right across to the far west of the island. The best place to appreciate the almond blossoms in all their splendour is on the Llucmajor plain. In March, the cherry trees are in flower, as are the apricot, apple and pear trees. By May summer is already in the air and red poppies stand out proudly against the cornflowers, daisies and wild orchids, while the lizards try out their new tails and the nightingales sing to the mountains. The cicadas bide their time until June before making their voices heard. Before you know it, it's high season again!

Mallorca has something for everyone. Each season has its own magical qualities; it's up to you to decide on which time of year suits you best. As for where you go in Mallorca, again, it depends on the type of break you're looking for. You can opt for the peace of inland villages, the unspoilt beauty of the northern coast, or you can go for the good old sun, sand and sangria-style holiday on the Palma coast. You can participate in all kinds of activities: water sports, tennis, horse-riding, golf, hiking, climbing, cycling and yachting. If it's pure relaxation you're after, you can laze about on the beach by day and get your exercise at one of the discos by night. Accommodation-wise, Mallorca has hotels of every category and for every budget . Alternatively, there are apartments sleeping one to five, monasteries offering tranquil seclusion, private holiday homes or even boats. Crowds or solitude, hustle and bustle, or peace and quiet, the choice is yours. And that's what makes Mallorca so great!

Olive groves like this one cover some 14 000 hectares of the island

Churches, windmills and watchtowers

The Balearic Islands played a vital role in the development of the Catalan culture

Archduke – Arxiduc

Ludwig Salvator, Archduke of Austria, son of Leopold II of Tuscany, was born in Florence in 1847. He first came to Mallorca in 1867, after his father fled Garibaldi's freedom fighters. This made Ludwig Salvator heir to a throne that no longer existed and gave him the chance to devote himself to his studies – natural history, geography and languages, his first love. His first trip to Mallorca to study the insect life of the island was by no means to be his last. A restless spirit led the archduke to visit many Mediterranean lands over a period of years, but the stretch of coast between Valldemossa and Deià always drew him back and eventually he was able to buy his own small 'empire' of estates in the area. In 1897, he finally settled down on his Son Marroig estate above the S'Estaca villa, which he had built for his companion, Catalina Homar, a carpenter's daughter from Valldemossa. His

most important work was published in the same year. The seven-volume *Balearics in Word and Picture* proved to be very influential in bringing Mallorca and the other islands of the archipelago to the attention of the European intelligentsia. He was granted honorary citizenship by the Mallorcan authorities in 1910 but, with the outbreak of war in 1914, he was forced to return to Vienna. He died on 12 October 1915 in Schloss Brandeis near Prague. Known to the Mallorcans simply as the Arxiduc, Ludwig Salvator made a great contribution to the study of Mallorca and is remembered fondly on the island to this day.

Balearic Islands

The Balearic Islands got their name from the *baliarides* (from the Greek *ballein,* meaning to throw). They were Mallorcan sling-shot troops, feared mercenaries who fought on the battlefields in ancient times. They took part in the Roman campaign of 146 BC that led to the destruction of Carthage. The Balearic archipelago is made up of 151 islands and has a total land surface area

A restored windmill near Llucmajor - not that the wind will turn this one's blades!

of approximately 5000 square metres. Mallorca, with 3648 square metres and a population of 595 000, is the largest island in the group. The other main islands are Menorca, Ibiza and Formentera. The remaining 147 islands are uninhabited. The archipelago is one of the 17 regions of Spain - the Comunitat Autónoma de les Illes Balears (the Autonomous Balearic Region) - and is governed from Palma, the regional capital.

In terms of population, this is the fourth largest Spanish region, with 740 000 inhabitants, with the highest income per capita.

Català (Catalan)

Català is not a dialect but a language in its own right. Like Castillian (the language the rest of the world calls Spanish), Italian, French and Portuguese, Catalan evolved from Vulgar Latin and, during the 13th century, it became a written language thanks to the efforts of the philosopher, poet and missionary Ramón Llull (Raimundus Lullus). Today the Catalan language is spoken in the Catalan regions on both sides of the Pyrenees, in Valencia, Andorra and parts of Aragón, in Alghero on the island of Sardinia and on the Balearic Islands. Mallorquí (Mallorcan) is a dialect of Catalan, as are Menorquí and Ibizenc, the dialects spoken on Menorca and Ibiza respectively.

Both Catalan and Castillian enjoy the same legal status on Mallorca and in the rest of the Balearic region. This was not always the case. During the long period under Franco's rule, the strict centralist policies imposed

by the dictator meant that only Castillian could be regarded as the official language for the whole of Spain. This law was strictly enforced and attempts, often brutal and violent, were made to suppress Catalan and other Iberian languages like Galician and Basque.

With the establishment of democracy and the subsequent recognition of the Balearic region as autonomous, Catalan speakers began to fight back. This reinstatement of the language is immediately evident to any first-time visitor. All street and place names have been renamed in Catalan. In Palma alone, between 200 and 300 streets are renamed each year – *calle* (street in Castillian) for example, becomes *carrer* and *plaza* (square) is changed to *plaça*. The names of various villages and towns are also still in the process of being changed – Pollensa is now Pollença, Santa Margerita has resumed its original name of Santa Margalida, Puerto de Alcúdia has been transformed into Port d'Alcúdia and El Arenal has become S'Arenal or L'Arenal. This latter is a very good example of the conflict that has arisen between Mallorquinists and Catalanists. There is a disagreement about whether the Mallorcan definite article 's' or the Catalan article 'l' should be adopted. Fanatics on both sides run around with cans of spray-paint 'correcting' the signs and street names, with the inevitable result that it is almost impossible to make out what was on the sign in the first place. Another point to bear in mind is that not all Mallorcans speak Mallorquí or Catalá, as one in four inhabitants comes from the mainland, mostly from Andalucia in southern Spain. Spanish (Castillian) is the language spoken there and interestingly enough all four Mallorcan daily papers are published in Castillian.

Don't be afraid to try out your Spanish – the Mallorcans appreciate any attempt to speak it and if you show some interest in learning at least the Catalan for hello and thank you, you're bound to get a positive reaction with plenty of people being willing to teach you more. In the coastal resorts, you'll find that you can get by with English or German, particularly when talking to younger people. The schools here give lessons in both Castillian and Catalan and the first choice when it comes to a third language is English.

The spelling of place names in this guide is based on an official list published in Spring 1995 and therefore corresponds to the currently accepted norm. So, if you compare this guide to previously published guides or older maps, you may well see place or street names spelt differently. In some cases, the Castillian name is still given, for example Playa de Palma and Castillo del Rey, because these are the names the Mallorquins themselves use.

Churches

Dedicated church enthusiasts will have some difficulty in indulging their passion on Mallorca. Most of the one hundred or so churches on the island are accessible only during services. It has to be said that many of the churches themselves and their contents are fairly uninspiring.

They are appreciated for their honest provincial charm rather than for any great artistic or architectural merit. The occasional brightly painted Madonna and skilfully carved crucifix are worth a closer look, as are some of the prayer-houses dating from the time of the re-establishment of Christianity in the 13th century. Most of these prayer-houses are no longer used for services, having been superseded by larger, more modern churches, with their imposing bell towers. The most impressive bell tower on the island belongs to the parish church at Sencelles.

Countryside and People

For those who want to explore more of the countryside and get to know the local people better, there are plenty of opportunities to do so. It is possible to venture around the island on foot, by car or even by bike. In recent years, off-road vehicles have become popular and there are a number of organized 'jeep safaris' you can go on. However, a number of people have been hiring jeeps to explore the island for themselves, sometimes driving across private land without the landowner's permission. Groups of hikers have also taken to walking across private land. Consequently, landowners have been forced to prohibit access to their land in a number of cases, and this arrogance on the part of holiday-makers has sometimes led to uneasy relationships between tourists and the local people. If you are polite and ask permission to walk through private land, however, then it's unlikely you'll be refused.

The language does create a barrier which makes it difficult to get to know the locals. Mallorquí is virtually incomprehensible to the non-native and the further inland you get the less English or German is understood. That's why, if you want to make even the briefest contact with the locals, it's vital to have some knowledge of Spanish, if only for the sake of politeness. You are also more likely to be successful in getting a friendly response if you are on your own or at most in twos or threes. On the whole, large groups are not very welcome.

Crime

Petty theft constitutes 85% of all crimes on Mallorca, committed, in the main, by drug-users. Tourists are the prime targets as they stand out, mainly because of their clothing, and are easy prey. Most tourists take the precaution of carrying their valuables around with them, but this isn't necessarily the best thing to do. When in holiday mood, it is easy to become careless. Cameras and clothes with documents left lying around are easy pickings. To lessen the likelihood of your becoming a victim of theft, here are a few simple precautions you should take: leave all valuables, including passports, in the hotel safe; don't leave valuable items in clear view in a car; don't carry your wallet or handbag with documents, credit cards, etc. unless you need them; don't carry more money than you really need and just try and keep your wits about you. If all this sounds a bit gloomy, then it's worth remembering that street crime is in fact much rarer on Mallorca than in other popular European holiday destinations. Wherever there are tourists there will be theft, so it's better to be safe than sorry.

Economy

The Mallorcan economy is heavily dependent on tourism, industry and crafts, as well as agriculture and fishing. Of the three main sectors, tourism provides about 70% of the gross national product, with industry and crafts providing 24% and the remaining 6% coming from agriculture and fishing.

Agriculture is really only profitable when there is a good and efficient irrigation system in place. Yet only about 20 000 hectares of Mallorca is well irrigated. The remaining arable land is cultivated with almond, lemon and orange trees and olive groves which thrive in dry soil. The almond market faces strong competition from California and Valencia and the olive oil business is suffering because the high acid content of the oil produced does not meet EU standards, which means it cannot be exported. The fruit of the carob tree is no longer required by the paper and pharmaceutical industries, at one time mainstays of this particular branch of agriculture. Farmers have been forced to tighten their belts and reduce the acreage planted, which has meant that the number of vineyards in particular has been drastically reduced. In 1925, some 30 000 hectares were covered by vines, but by 1993 only 700 hectares of vineyards had survived.

Livestock farming has fared relatively well, mainly because its by-products – milk, eggs and

Lavishly decorated altar in the Finca Son March

natural beauty and temperate climate draw millions of people each year. One of the main sources of employment on the island is the manufacture of souvenirs, and from 1964 to 1994 the number of people employed in related service industries rose from 34% to 76% of the workforce. The number of young people seeking employment in and around Palma has resulted in the population of the city doubling, rising from 160 000 in 1960 to the 318 000 residents it has today. More than 38 000 people live and work in the resort areas of Palmanova, Magaluf, Santa Ponça and Peguera – thirty years ago it was only 6000.

wool – contribute around 15 billion pesetas a year to the local economy. Traditional fishing has been hit hard, but attempts are being made to compensate for this with the introduction of fish farming. The initial experiments in this area have produced some quite encouraging results.

There is no heavy industry as such on Mallorca, apart from the cement works at Lloseta where 90% of the building materials required for construction on the island are produced. There is also a thriving soft-drink and mineral water industry which produces several million litres per annum. Other industry tends to be small scale, mainly revolving around the production of leather goods and shoes, artificial pearls and jewellery, ceramics, especially tiles, and hand-made goods. Because of its location, however, Mallorca is at a disadvantage when it comes to exporting its manufactured goods, because the cost of transportation is so high.

But when it comes to the tourist industry itself, the location couldn't be better. Mallorca's

Excavations

There is little left in the way of remains for archaeologists to excavate on Mallorca. Apart from a few shards of pottery, the Phoenicians and Greeks didn't leave much of substance behind them. The only concrete evidence of the Roman period remaining intact today is the bridge at Pollença. Excavations at Pollentia and the Teatro Romano near Alcúdia haven't unearthed much of significance apart from the foundation walls. During the Dark Ages the island was dominated by Vandals, Byzantines and Franks, who left nothing in the way of architecture; nor is there much of interest from the Moorish period – the Arabian buildings were either destroyed or incorporated into Christian architecture. There are, however, some remains of Bronze Age megaliths *(talayots)*, dating from about 2000 BC. These can be found near Artà, Capicorp Vell and to the south of

Ses Salines. On the outskirts of Can Picafort there is a vast necropolis, with graves from the late Bronze Age and the early period of Phoenician settlement. Entrance to most of the excavation sites is free of charge.

Junípero Serra

The man Americans have to thank for half a dozen of their largest cities, Fray Junípero Serra, was born in Petra on 24 November 1713. As a young man he joined the Franciscan order and gained his doctorate in theology and philosophy at the age of 27. In 1749, he and four other members of the order travelled to Mexico to carry out missionary work there, moving later to California. Not content with just preaching, the young Franciscan introduced the latest agricultural methods to the local people, and taught them how to read and write. He established a number of mission stations which he named after various saints and holy places honoured on his home island – San Diego, Santa Barbara, San Carlos and Los Angeles. In 1776, he founded the Dolores mission, which grew into one of the most beautiful cities in the USA, San Francisco.

The 'Californian Apostle' died on 28 August 1783 and was buried in his mission headquarters at San Carlos, not far from where Hollywood stands today. He left behind him 21 self-sufficient and self-supporting communities. He was canonized by Pope John Paul II in September 1988 and there is a bronze statue of him in front of the Cathedral in Palma. You can visit the house where he was born and there is a small museum which is dedicated to him in Petra.

Media

There are four daily newspapers published in Palma, with a total circulation of about 100 000. You can also get the major European and Arabic papers at kiosks in the capital and in most of the holiday resorts. In the so-called '*part forana*' – the hinterland – around 50 or so local papers are published each week. These papers are written in Mallorquí and they have a total circulation of about 50 000. The oldest local newspaper, *Sóller,* first appeared in the town of the same name in 1885.

Mallorca's English daily paper, the *Daily Bulletin,* celebrated its 30th anniversary in 1993 and the German-language weekly, *Mallorca-Magazin,* first published in 1972, is still going strong. You can also get English programmes on the radio. Antena 3 (106.1 FM) broadcasts chat and music shows daily with news bulletins covering both local and international events. All the larger hotels have satellite TV, but English books are hard to find, with only some kiosks and the larger bookshops in Palma stocking them.

Ramón Llull

Raimundus Lullus, as he was known to medieval scholars, is considered to be the father of the Catalan language. He wrote the vast majority of his works in the language, and his novel *Blanquera,* about a Utopian state on earth, is thought to be the first European novel to introduce character development to the genre.

Ramón Llull, the son of a Catalan noble, was born in about 1232 in Palma. A career at court was his noble birthright, but he turned this down and opted instead for a life of contemplation. When he was 30 he went to live as a hermit on Mount Randa and later lived in the remoter part of the island on the north-west coast. Here, in the royal hunting lodge at Miramar, he founded a language school for future missionaries, who were taught Arabic, Hebrew and Turkish, so that they could preach to 'heathens' and show them the error of their ways in their own tongue. But Llull was no narrow-minded bigot. He believed that the spirit of the Levant could be combined with the acumen of the West to create a fruitful and peaceful cooperation between Jews, Muslims and Christians around the world, for the benefit of all mankind. In his book *Ars magna* he described this synthesis as he saw it. He also invented his own system of numerology to try and demonstrate the workings of the human mind. In this respect, he could also be considered as one of the forefathers of modern cybernetics. He spent the last 30 years of his life travelling the world as one of 'God's knights', teaching, preaching and carrying out missionary work. He is said to have died in 1335 on board a ship that was bringing him back to Mallorca from North Africa. He was buried in the Monastery church of San Francisco in Palma.

Robert Graves

Robert Graves, the English poet and author, spent most of his life in Mallorca, where he wrote his most famous work *I, Claudius*. He first arrived on the island in 1929, accompanied by Laura Riding, his American mistress. They decided to settle in Deià, a small town north of Palma, not far from Valldemossa. The stark yet breathtaking landscape of mountains, sea and grey rock was a spectacular setting to which Graves returned over and over throughout his life. The success of his autobiographical work *Goodbye To All That*, about his experiences during the First World War, enabled them to move to a beautiful house perched on the mountainside on the far side of Deià, with a vertiginous drop to the sea down below. Graves returned to this house with his second wife, Beryl, and their children in 1946 and became known to the locals as the 'Grand Old Man of Deià'. He fiercely defended this area against tourist development. He is buried in the town cemetery and his grave is marked with the simple epitaph 'Robert Graves, Poeta, 1895-1985'.

His son, William Graves, has written a book about his family life on Mallorca called *Wild Olives, Life in Majorca with Robert Graves*. The house itself isn't open to the public because the family still lives there, but the hilltop town of Deià (see p. 53) is well worth a visit to see the place from which Graves drew so much inspiration.

Santa Catalina Tomás

The Mallorcans have a special place in their hearts for their patron saint, St Catalina (Catherine). She is greatly admired and often referred to as *beateta,* which is the familiar form of *beata,* meaning holy one. The Mallorcans have always felt her to be one of them, even after she was elevated to sainthood by Pope Pius XI in 1930.

Catalina Tomás was born on 1 May 1531, the daughter of a farmer in Valldemossa. She worked as a maid until she entered the Augustinian Order at the age of 21. She was quick and intelligent and very soon she began to exercise an influence in church politics, particularly in connection with the Council of Trent. The viceroy, Don Guillem Rocafull, fondly referred to her as 'God's secretary', but when her fellow nuns tried to make her Mother Superior, she rejected their offer vehemently, preferring to remain a simple nun. She died in 1574 at the age of 43 and was buried in her convent chapel at Santa Maria Magdalena in Palma. Nearly 450 years later, her body is still in a state of almost perfect preservation. Opposite the house where she was born in Valldemossa stands a statue of her. A fresh-water spring emerges from her feet. To her followers, this is the living proof that their *beateta* really is the blessed saint of serving maids.

Turkish Towers

During the 16th century, Moorish pirates increased the number and ferocity of their raids on Mallorca. To defend themselves, the islanders not only built fortified castles at towns like Artá and Capdepera, but also erected watchtowers along the coastline, called *atalayas,* or 'Turkish Towers'. They were large enough to provide quarters for a ten-man watch company. Smoke signals during the day and torches at night were used to warn of an approaching pirate raid. The system was so effective that it took only 10 minutes from the initial signal for the defenders to be ready at their posts and for the message to be passed to the headquarters at Palma. The Spanish word *atalaya* comes from the Arabic *atalayi,* meaning 'watch' or 'guard', as does the term *talayot,* used to describe the defensive watch towers found in the Bronze-Age settlements. Most of the remaining *atalayas* have been converted into viewpoints for visitors.

Water

Water supply on the island is dependent on rainfall. The average annual rainfall of 300 billion litres is sufficient for one year's water supply to the island. Of course, if the rainfall is below average, then there is the threat of drought, which doesn't on the whole affect tourists as much as it does farmers, who use around 70% of the total supply. Only 5% is used up by tourism, the remaining 25% being used by the domestic market. Mallorca's reservoirs and pipe-lines are in dire need of modernization. Every year around 40 million cubic metres of perfectly good drinking water is wasted as it flows from the Serra del Nord mountains straight into the sea.

Windmills

Windmills are as much a symbol of Mallorca as the Eiffel Tower is of Paris. They are a popular subject for photographers and there can't be many people who have been to Mallorca who don't have a picture of a windmill somewhere amongst their holiday snaps. Most of the windmills are to be found on the Sant Jordí plain, their huge blades powering the machinery that brings the water from the subterranean water table to the surface. Each sweep of the blades raises some 25 litres of water from a depth of about 25 m. With 20 full cycles per minute, this means that approximately 3000 litres are brought to the surface every hour. The water is stored initially in tanks, to be used as required for irrigation in the fields. A number of these windmills (*molinos*) are no longer active, having been replaced by diesel-driven and electric pumps, and so have fallen into disrepair. An association was founded in 1975, the 'Asociación de amigos de los molinos', with the aim of preserving as many of the mills as possible. They have had a certain amount of success, and recently a small number of the old flour mills have even been reactivated. It looks as if the Mallorcan windmill, a classic national symbol, is in safe hands, for the foreseeable future at least.

Xenophobia

The Greek word *xenos* has two meanings – stranger and guest. Initially, tourists were made to feel very welcome in Mediterranean countries. The differences in outlook and custom intrigued the inhabitants, who were on the whole curious about tourists who wanted to visit their country. At first *Xenophilia,* the liking of foreigners, was the general attitude towards tourists, not least because they brought money into the country and created new employment. Gradually, this attitude changed for the worse. The rela-

tionship between tourist and local, paying guest and serving host, is by its nature artificial and the inevitable clash of cultures caused resentment. On the bad side, you have the ignorant tourist who makes no effort to understand the culture and language of his host country, or who doesn't even have the slightest wish to experience what the country has to offer. These are the people who want English beer, bacon and eggs, or fish and chips wherever they go. They are often rude, upset local sensibilities and behave in a manner that is quite unacceptable, from not respecting local dress customs to outrageous behaviour when drunk. Small wonder that the locals who have to deal with this type of tourist often treat them with contempt and as a result, all tourists are tarred with the same brush . . . this is when xenophilia turns into xenophobia. This is what has happened to a certain extent on Mallorca, where tourists are no longer regarded as guests but as money-making machines, who are lumped into one of two categories: 'quality tourists' or 'cheap holiday-makers'. Some islanders have quickly learned how to rip off the lager louts and hooligans who give other tourists a bad name, treatment which many Mallorcans feel they deserve.

However, all is not lost. If you treat the islanders with courtesy and respect and show willing to learn at least some of the language, then you'll find you get a completely different reaction from them. They are by nature very friendly people and will do everything they can to make your stay on their island a happy one.

Mallorcan cuisine

Mallorcan cuisine is earthy and delicious and holds its own against the world's best

When it comes to food, there's certainly no shortage of choice in Mallorca. All tastes and budgets are catered for, from international gourmet restaurants to the inevitable fast-food outlets like McDonalds and Wimpy. The major world cuisines are comprehensively represented on the island, and you can find French, German, Italian, Chinese, Japanese, Moroccan and Lebanese food among others. You can sample different Spanish regional dishes in the many restaurants offering Basque, Galician, Catalan and Andalusian specialities. Considering the size of the island, the variety on offer is astounding. But all this doesn't mean that Mallorca's native cuisine has been forgotten. There are plenty of restaurants specializing in good wholesome Mallorcan food. *La cuina mallorquina* is simple and traditional. On a typical menu you would find a choice of pork, lamb, chicken or fish dishes and

there is usually a stew of some description on offer. All dishes are generally served with *salsa mallorquina* (a Mallorcan sauce) and of course *pamboli (pa amb oli,* bread with olive oil), without which no Mallorcan meal would be complete. The island cuisine may not have many frills but it is nonetheless delicious and surprisingly subtle in flavour.

The growth in tourism has led to more and more international restaurants being opened in Palma and the resorts, which has meant that the number of restaurants serving traditional Mallorcan food has decreased and Mallorcan cuisine has been pushed out of the capital to the remoter areas. For many of today's more discerning tourists, however, local cooking is an essential part of the holiday experience. There are plenty of authentic Mallorcan restaurants inland if you venture to towns such as Inca, Sineu and Algaida. If you're staying in Palma there are still a few good Mallorcan restaurants to be found if you look hard enough. They serve basic fare, but are unpretentious and good value for money .

Skilled hands create the sweet and sour pastry which Mallorcans are so fond of

The Menu

The standard menu has a dozen or so Mallorcan specialities on offer. For a real Mallorcan dish try *Sopa mallorquina,* which is made up of thinly sliced rustic bread heated in the oven until nice and crisp, then soaked in a vegetable broth and covered in cauliflower, cabbage and whatever other vegetables are in season. Most menus include some kind of soup, the traditional flavours being *sopa de guisantes,* pea soup, *sopa de verdura,* vegetable soup, the ingredients of which vary according to the season, and *sopa de pescado,* fish soup, whose contents again depend on what is available or whatever has been caught. *Caldo* is consommé made from either meat, fish or chicken stock.

A typical 'peasant' dish is *arroz brut,* or 'coarse rice', a type of risotto typically made with saffron rice, strips of pork or rabbit, and mixed vegetables. *Arroz a la marinera* is the same dish made with fish or shellfish instead of meat. As you can imagine, these rice-based dishes leave a lot of scope for the chef to add whatever takes his fancy or whatever he has available – perhaps some quail, pigeon or some kind of game. This means that no matter how often you decide to have risotto, you'll never get the same dish twice.

No Mallorcan menu would be complete without the tasty *frito mallorquín* - fresh offal, preferably mutton or lamb, which is fried with potatoes, onions, garlic, fennel and paprika.

Tumbet is an ideal summer dish – a concoction of aubergines, courgettes, potatoes, onions and paprika. It is often served with a fillet of fish or veal, in which case it's called *tumbet con pescado* or *tumbet con carne.* The truly authentic restaurants will cook all of these casserole dishes in an *olla,* the bulbous clay pot used in traditional Mallorcan cooking.

Pork or lamb are the meats most often used in Mallorcan cooking. Mallorcan lamb is usually of an excellent quality but sometimes, during the long hot summer months, it can lose some of its flavour, so at this time of year you may be better off avoiding the *costillas de cordero* (lamb cutlets). If you want to be on the safe side, stick to pork dishes in summer such as *lomo con col,* pork escalopes lightly simmered in a *greixonera,* a shallow earthenware bowl, accompanied by cabbage stuffed with raisins, pine kernels and sausage. *Palomo con col* is a dish prepared in exactly the same way using pigeon instead of pork. *Lechona,* suckling pig, is considered a real delicacy and is usually only served on special occasions. *Pollo,* chicken, turns up on practically every menu but it is not usually cooked in a very imaginative way and, apart from the fact that the chickens are usually free-range and therefore more succulent, these chicken dishes are nothing out of the ordinary. Other highlights of Mallorcan cuisine include salami-like sausages made of pure pork, such as *sobrasada,* which is spiced with paprika, and *butifarra,* which is very similar to black pudding.

Paella, which originates from Valencia and *gazpacho,* the ice-cold garlic and tomato soup from Andalusia, have become an integral part of the Mallorcan diet and are on the menu in the ma-

On the house?

You find your restaurant, take your seat, and are pleasantly surprised to find the waiter hurrying over to fill your glass with a welcoming drink. But how do you know whether it's on the house? If it is free of charge then the waiter will say *de la casa* as he is filling your glass. If, on the other hand, he asks whether you care for an aperitif, and you say yes, you will find that the cost of the drink will be added to your bill. And another thing – if you want music, then you usually have to pay for it.

jority of Spanish and Mallorcan restaurants. They are often better prepared here than in their native regions. Unfortunately, the same can't be said about other culinary imports such as pizza and pasta which all too often taste nothing like the real thing.

On the whole Mallorcan fish restaurants, which are concentrated in the coastal regions and Palma, are good and offer a wide range of seafood dishes, from fresh lobster to mussels and from *pescado a la sal* (salted fish) to deep-fried sardines. But the local fishing industry cannot keep up with demand. Fresh fish is mostly flown in from the Spanish Atlantic regions, Galicia and the Canary Islands which makes it expensive. Chances are the crayfish on your plate will have started life in Singapore! Frozen fish is often used, though this isn't necessarily a problem with squid *(calamares),* cuttlefish *(sepias),* and octopus *(pulpos).* A good fish restaurant will have a separate section on the menu for fresh fish – *pescado fresco.* Unfortunately, this doesn't guarantee the freshness of the tartare sauce or of the homemade garlic sauce, *aioli,* which Mallorcans love to use as an accompaniment to white fish or snails. You have to be a little bit careful during the

summer months, as these sauces can quickly turn in the heat.

Dining Mallorcan-style

If you want to dine like the locals, then there is a simple rule to follow – eat lots, talk lots and drink moderately. Mallorcan people love to have a good, lively conversation over dinner and will never hurry their food. Mealtimes are important social occasions, when friends and family gather together around the table.

Breakfast *(desayuno)* is the same as it is in most Mediterranean countries. It is a simple affair consisting of a *café sólo* (espresso), a *cortado* (espresso with milk), or a *café con leche* (white coffee) accompanied by a *croasante* (croissant), an *ensaimada* (a sweet pastry), or a *bocadillo* (a cheese or ham roll). It's perfectly acceptable to dunk your croissant in your coffee if you want to.

If you're feeling peckish between meals, you can pick up some freshly made *bunyols* – small round deep-fried doughnuts dipped in sugar – from one of the many roadside stalls dotted around most towns.

During the week, lunch is not generally a grand affair, unless it's some kind of business lunch. But come Sunday, or any holiday, lunch (*almuerzo*) and dinner (*cena*) are the highlight of the day. These meals are several courses long, and can last for hours. The marathon kicks off with assorted nibbles (*para picar*) followed by a selection of starters which might include snails, shrimps or finely-sliced squid (*pica-pica*) in a savoury sauce, a choice of cheeses, salamis, hams, radishes and pâtés. All these are accompanied by the ever-present bread and olives. And that's just the beginning. Now it's time to study the main menu. This is a long drawn-out process, involving plenty of discussion, probably a little argument and finding out what the children want before finally settling on what you want to order.

A typical restaurant meal consists of three courses: *entremés,* starter, also known as the *primer plato*, the *plato segundo*, main course, and *postre,* dessert. For a starter, you can choose between salad, *ensaladas,* or *sopa,* either a bowl of *caldo* or a plate of *arroz brut.* The main course usually consists of red meat, fish or poul-

try. Side dishes, *guarnición,* and vegetables have to be ordered separately and they can be found in the menu under the heading *Verduras.* For dessert, you can choose between cheese, fruit, ice-cream or *flan,* which is a type of creme caramel, followed by a *café solo* and a Spanish brandy or *coñac.* In Galician restaurants a popular alternative to brandy is *aguardiente,* a strong spirit. If you feel like splashing out, you can always order a bottle of Catalonian sparkling wine (*champan*) a selection of which you'll find on the wine list under 'Cava'.

In general, the Spaniards and Mallorcans eat late. Lunch doesn't usually start until 2 p.m. and in summer this can be an hour later. The evening meal doesn't normally start until about 9 p.m., again in summer this can be as late as 10.30 or 11 p.m. Most of the good restaurants don't even open until around 9 p.m. and it is customary to book your table in advance. If you only want something light, like a salad, then it's best to go to a *bodega,* a *celler,* a *cafe-*

The 'Theatre Bakery' in Palma has delicious snacks for all tastes

26

teria or a bar that serves food. These places are a little less formal and you don't have to eat a full three or four course meal.

One of the best things about Spain is the *tapas* tradition. *Tapas* are bite-sized snacks served on small plates called *platitos. Tapas* come in all shapes and sizes. The classic tapa is *tortilla,* a delicious potato and onion omelette eaten cold. But this is just one among countless possibilities: mushrooms, olives, fried sardines, mussels, peppers, meat balls, potato salad with peas and boiled egg, Basque and Galician specialities like *salpicón,* a savoury salad with fish and shellfish, or *calamares en su tinta,* squid in its own ink. If you have trouble choosing, you can order a *tapa combinada,* which is a plate that has a little bit of everything.

The bill is presented to just one person and there is no point in asking for a separate bill. This will only lead to confusion and mistakes being made. It's customary to add a 10% tip or *propina.*

Drink

If the statistics are to be believed, then Spain, which includes Mallorca, takes second place behind France and is just ahead of Italy as having the highest level of alcohol consumption in Europe. It's surprising, therefore, that you very rarely see a Spaniard the worse for drink in public. Wine is thought of as part and parcel of a meal and it is not usually drunk outside mealtimes. The concept of spending an evening drinking in a pub, without eating any food, is an alien one to most Spaniards.

Most of the wines that appear on the wine list are brought over from mainland Spain - from La Rioja, Catalonia, Navarra and Galicia. They are lighter and fresher than the heavier Mallorcan wines, which admittedly go very well with the local food. The red wines produced on the island have an alcohol content of between 12 and 14%, while the whites and rosés come in at about 11 to 12.5%. With the arrival of tourists and their drinking habits, the Mallorcans developed a taste for beer (*cerveza*) and many bars and restaurants now serve beer on draught. English, German and Spanish bottled beers are available just about everywhere and *cerveza* is now almost as popular as wine as a mealtime drink.

But the amount of wine or beer drunk with a meal is not the main reason for the high level of alcohol consumption in Spain. The custom of the *copa,* where friends and businessmen meet for a quick sherry, liqueur or cognac, has a lot to do with the figures. A good bar will stock all of the most popular European drinks from Campari or Martini to Scotch whisky, gin and vodka. The array of Spanish cognacs displayed behind the bar is astounding, and if you like brandy it's worth sampling one or two of the better brands. Spanish cognac can now officially be referred to as brandy thanks to recent EU legislation.

It's not all that common to toast someone's health in Spain, except on special occasions, such as someone's birthday or saint's day. On these occasions, the usual toast is simply *'Salut!'* which means 'Good health!'. If a toast is proposed during a meal the traditional cry is *'Bon profit!'* which means 'Prosperity!'.

Arts and crafts

Woodwork and artwork, leather and lace,
capers and ceramics – all made in Mallorca

Ninety out of every hundred souvenirs bought on Mallorca are actually produced on the island. The majority of these souvenirs are ornaments and, ironically, 'Andalusian' fans and castanets. On closer inspection, you will notice that most of these goods carry the inscription 'Made in Manacor'.

Manacor is not only the centre of the Mallorcan souvenir industry but also home to the island's pearl industry. Mallorcan pearls are artificial, but are made from natural products – glass beads with a mother-of-pearl coating. After the pearls are coated, they are all polished by hand. Mallorcan pearls are extremely durable and hard-wearing and are resistant to cold, heat, perspiration and cosmetics. Each item bears a red sticker which indicates that they are guaranteed for 10 years. They are an excellent substitute for natural oyster pearls and make a great gift or souvenir, suitable for everyday wear.

A colourful scene in the lively market town of Inca

Mallorcan ceramics make some of the best souvenirs. Pottery is an ancient craft still practised on the island. The original workshops (*alfarerías*) date back to the Arabic period. Today, most of Mallorca's potters (*ollers*) live and work in Pórtol, a town about 15 km north-east of Palma. It's possible to visit some of the workshops and watch the skilled craftsmen at work. Although most workshops are now fitted with modern machinery, the same fundamental techniques are still applied in the making of traditional ceramics.

There are two basic earthenware containers found in the average Mallorcan household. The *olla* is a typical clay pot that comes in all shapes and sizes and is used to store just about everything from spices and grain to the ashes of some dear departed! The *greixonera* is a traditional cooking vessel that is very heat-resistant and can be placed directly over a naked flame without breaking. The pots are glazed on the inside and fired in a kiln. The same is true of all the ceramic plates and jugs that are in everyday use on

A glorious display of traditional pottery in Manacor

Mallorca. There is something timeless about these utensils and you really get the feeling that you are living a little bit of history when you use them. Not only do they make great souvenirs, but they are practical and will last you a long time. Prices vary according to size, ranging from about 400 to 8000 pesetas.

There is another ceramic manufacturing centre not far from Pórtol, where the craftsmen concentrate on making *siurrells*. These are white clay figures, traditionally painted red and green, which range in size from 10 to 100 cm. Their shape is reminiscent of archaic figures from Crete and Sardinia. They are always depicted standing, never sitting, and have an in-built flute that produces a rather shrill sound when you blow into it. You can also get animal *siurrells* – bulls with marvellously convoluted horns, dogs, horses and peacocks. There is an annual *siurrell* market held in Marratxí towards the end of June where you can see row upon row of these strange creations.

Apart from the pearl and ceramic industries, another traditional craft which is still thriving on the island is glass-blowing. There are three authentic workshops – Vidrios Gordiola near Algaida, La Menestralía near Campanet and La Fiore near S'Esgleieta on the road from Palma to Valldemossa. Traditional methods are still used in glass manufacture and it is fascinating to watch the skilled craftsmen at work, creating beautiful objects before your very eyes.

Apart from the distinctive ceramics, pearls and hand-blown glass, there really isn't very much on Mallorca that can't be found elsewhere. Palma has the same sort of shops you would expect to find in any major European city, but it does have the reputation of being the most expensive place to buy textiles in Spain. If it's clothes you're after and you're not all that bothered about buying up-to-the-minute fashion, the sales (*rebajas*) are worth waiting for. There's many a bargain to be had and you can find top-quality merchandise at reductions of up to 50%. The summer sales begin just before summer itself and the winter sales start on 6 December, St Nicholas' Day.

Shoes made in Spain and on the island are always a good buy, but you have to be a bit careful when buying other leather goods. Although Mallorca has a worldwide reputation for its leather, quality is not always guaranteed. Real bargains are the exception rather than the rule and styles can be a bit old-fashioned.

If you take a detour through some of the back streets in Palma, it is still possible to come across genuine Mallorcan articles that have disappeared from the larger shops and department stores. If you look carefully you can find authentic lace and crochet work. These exquisite pieces are handmade in the villages and decorated with the traditional Mallorcan *llengua* (tongue) pattern. They usually come in a wide variety of colours and designs.

Mallorca is not the best place for antiques, but it is a major centre for modern and contemporary art – a good place for those who are interested in buying or just looking. There are more than 50 galleries in Palma and other towns such as Sineu, Pollença and Deià, that exhibit contemporary works mainly by Mallorcan and Catalan artists. The styles are varied and you can find conventional landscape alongside avant-garde and abstract works.

The local street markets, held weekly in all the major towns, sell the usual mixture of fresh produce, tourist paraphernalia and household goods. Keep an eye out for the kitchen knives which are manufactured on the island. Although they are quick to rust they are nice and sharp and make an unusual and practical souvenir.

If you're looking for something edible to bring back as a souvenir, then the best thing you can buy are the locally cultivated capers (*alcaparras*). These 'green pearls' from Felanitx, Sant Joan and Campos are reputedly the best in the world.

Festivals and processions

*Mallorcan festivals are a combination
of religious ceremony and riotous celebration*

There are about one hundred festivals celebrated each year on Mallorca. Being a Catholic country, many of these *festas* are religious in origin. They are usually held in honour of some patron saint or other and each community on the island celebrates its own saint's day. These festivals are a combination of solemn religious ceremony and fun and feasting. The *verbena* is the highpoint of any Mallorcan festival. It is the open-air celebration that takes place on the eve of the saint's day, with music, dancing, masked processions and firework displays. These *festas* can last for up to a week and during this period most businesses in the community are closed; post offices, banks, local authority offices and pharmacies stay open, however. The one exception to this is 25 July – Sant Jaume. James (San Jaime, San Diego, Santiago) is the patron saint of the whole of Spain and so this day is a public holiday for the whole country.

Ritual Semana Santa procession: one of the Easter highlights

PUBLIC HOLIDAYS

1 January: New Year's Day
6 January: Epiphany
March or April: Good Friday, Easter Monday
1 May: May Day
May or June: Corpus Christi
25 July: St James' Day (Sant Jaume)
15 August: Assumption
12 October: National Day *(Día de la Hispanidad)*
1 November: All Saints' Day
6 December: Constitution Day
8 December: Conception of the Blessed Virgin
25/26 December: Christmas

SAINTS' DAYS – PROCESSIONS – PILGRIMAGES

5 January
Cabalgada de los Reyes Magos. The Three Kings or Wise Men disembark in Palma's harbour and ride through the town; even the villages welcome the *Reyes Magos* who bring gifts for the children in a cart drawn by a donkey.

17 January
Sant Antoni and the blessing of household pets *(Ses Beneides).* In

the north and east of the island, a masked procession takes place at dusk which symbolizes the driving out of the devil.

20 January

Sant Sebastiá. A week-long festival in honour of the patron saint of Palma, St Sebastian – huge firework display on the eve of the actual saint's day.

Good Friday

Processió de la Sang. Some 4000 penitents take part in the Good Friday procession through Palma, while in Pollença, the ★ ❂ *Devallement* or lowering of the cross is celebrated.

Tuesday after Easter

Pilgrimage *(romería)* to the shrine of Our Lady at Lloseta, the oldest image on the island in the Ermita del Cocó, with music and dancing outside the settlement. In Mancor de la Vall, there is a *romería* in honour of Santa Lucía, the holy martyr from Syracuse, and patron saint of the blind. As you might expect, a number of blind and partially-sighted people take part in this pilgrimage.

29 June

Sant Pere (St Peter). A procession of ships in the harbours of Palma, Andratx and Alcúdia.

16 July

Nuestra Señora del Carmen. Week-long festival with processions of ships in the harbours of Andratx, Cala Figuera, Cala d'Or, Cala Ratjada, Sóller and Portocristo.

27 July

Santa Catalina Tomás. Week-long festival in Valldemossa in honour of the saint who was born there on 1 May 1531. Concerts in the Carthusian monastery.

First Sunday in September

Processió de la Beata in Santa Margalida in honour of Santa Catalina Tomás.

SECULAR FESTIVALS & FAIRS

Last week in March

(Fira del Fang) Ceramics fair in Marratxí.

End of April

Agricultural show in Sineu.

First half of May

❂ *Cristians i morus - Ses valentes dones.* Week-long festival in Sóller. Reconstruction of the aftermath of the battle between 'Christians and Moors' which took place on 11 May 1561, when the 'brave women' of Sóller fought alongside their menfolk to repel the Turkish pirates.

MARCO POLO SELECTION: FESTIVALS

1 Marxa des Güell a Lluc a peu
Walk from Palma to the Monastery at Lluc – part pilgrimage, part fitness excursion (page 35)

2 Devallement
The solemn procession of the 'Descent from the Cross' on Good Friday in Pollença is an impressive religious ceremony (page 34)

June/July

❧ Pop and Jazz Festivals in Palma. Open-air concert (*Cançons de la Mediterrània* – Songs of the Mediterranean) in the Parc de la Mar featuring musicians from all over the Mediterranean.

July/August

Chopin Festival in the Carthusian monastery at Valldemossa. Solo performances.

Last week in July

★ ❧ *Marxa des Güell a Lluc a peu.* Procession from the Bar Güell in Palma to the monastery at Lluc (48 km), where the Moreneta, the Black Virgin of the Mountains, is honoured. The *Marxa* procession, which has attracted as many as 50 000 participants, was revived by a patriotic bar owner in 1973. The reason for taking part in the walk is as much social as it is devotional. The rallying cry is 'Let's go to Lluc, let's go on foot and let's go as brothers!'. This is one of the best opportunities to get to know both the island and its people.

June/September

International Music Festival in Pollença. Soloists and chamber orchestras perform in the courtyard of the former Dominican monastery of Santo Domingo.

First two weeks in September

International Tourist Week. Cala Millor/Cala Bona. A successful attempt by the communities of Sant Llorenç and Son Servera, within whose boundaries the resorts of Cala Millor and Cala Bona lie, to integrate these resort communities into Mallorcan life. A mixture of religious and secu-

Folk dancing on the La Granja Estate near Esporles

lar festivity, solemn masses with sporting competitions, and the usual *verbena* - dancing, food and fireworks.

End of September to end of October

❧ Harvest Festivals: The Melon Festival (*Festa des Meló*) in Vilafranca; Wine Festival (*Festa des Vermar*) on the last Sunday in September in Binissalem; Black Sausage Festival (*Festa des Butifarró*) on the first Sunday in October in Sant Joan; *Festa des Bunyol* (*bunyol* is a small doughnut – see p. 25) on 30 October in Petra.

November

Dijous Bó ('Fat Thursday'), an important agricultural show and week-long festival in Inca.

31 December

Festa de L'Estandart (Flag Festival). The Mallorcan National Day, which is only really celebrated as a holiday in Palma. On 31 December 1229, King Jaime I of Aragon entered Palma after his resounding victory over the Moors.

Town and beach

Where the action is: two-thirds of all the hotels on Mallorca are clustered around the capital

Geographically, the south-west coastal region can be divided into two areas. This natural division is created by the landscape which changes from the wide, expansive sandy Bay of Palma in the east to the rugged, fjord-like coastline around the Andratx peninsula in the west.

Palma Cathedral, 'The Cathedral of Light', one of the most beautiful churches in all of Spain

In the eastern section of the bay, the boundaries of the city of Palma and the Playa (beach) de Palma have merged, and they now form one community which stretches over 5 km of sandy beach. The city borders have also extended to the west and encompass the resorts of Calamajor, Sant Agustí and Illetes. Continuing westwards through the built-up areas of Portals Nous and Bendinat, past the yacht marina at Puerto Portals, you'll come to the

Hotel and Restaurant Prices

Hotels
Category 1: £70 - £150
Category 2: £40 - £70
Category 3: £10 - £40
Prices per person for one night in a double room with breakfast

Restaurants
Category 1: from £50
Category 2: £30 - £50
Category 3: under £30
Prices per person for a three-course meal without drinks

Important abbreviations

Avda. *Avenida* (avenue)
C/. *Calle/Carrer* (street)
Ctra. *Carretera* (main road, major route)

ptas. *Pesetas*
s/n *sin número* (no number)
Urb. *Urbanización* (urban development)

popular holiday resorts on the Costa de Calviá – Palmanova, Magaluf, Santa Ponça, Peguera, Camp de Mar and Port d'Andratx. Sant Elm is situated on the most south-western point, with the rocky island of Sa Dragonera lying just offshore.

Heading inland, the rich agricultural land begins immediately after you leave the last houses behind on the outskirts of Palma. The airport is located in the plain just beyond Playa de Palma. Continuing around the bay, east of the airport, the 25-km stretch of coastline between S'Arenal and Cala Pí is less densely populated. To the west, directly behind the resorts on the Andratx peninsula, the land rises steeply through mainly wooded terrain on which orchards of fruit trees have been cultivated, to the mountain ranges of Galatzó (1026 m) and Esclop (926 m).

One of the most appealing aspects of this region lies in the fact that you can find unspoilt areas of great natural beauty so near the city and crowded resorts. It's not surprising that two-thirds of all the accommodation available to holiday-makers on Mallorca is concentrated between S'Arenal and Sant Elm. Many of the hotels on this coast are open all year round. Public transport between the resorts and Palma is quick and efficient. Visitors have everything they need here, both in summer and in winter. Life around here never slows down.

ANDRATX / PORT D'ANDRATX

The tourist trade is an important contribution to the local economy. The main attraction in Andratx is the weekly market which draws holiday-makers from neighbouring resorts. The harbour town of Port d'Andratx is about 5 km away from Andratx itself. The tourists who come here seem happy to manage without a 'proper' beach. The main bay, Cala Llamp, can be easily reached but many of the outlying bays and coves can only be reached by boat. There are relatively few hotels here and most visitors stay in either private villas or apartments. La Mola peninsula

This is what thousands of holidaymakers come to Mallorca in search of — sun, sea and sand

MARCO POLO SELECTION: PALMA AND THE SOUTH-WEST COAST

1 La Seo
The Cathedral in Palma is one of the finest in Spain (page 43)

2 Castillo Bellver
Great view of Palma from this medieval castle (page 43)

3 Miró Centre
Hundreds of Joan Miró's works are displayed in the museum (page 44)

4 Palma Old Town
Explore the back streets and admire the characteristic houses of the old town (page 42)

5 Galilea
Picturesque mountain village commanding a fine view of the South-West coastline (page 41)

6 Port d'Andratx
Beautiful harbour with a touch of Saint-Tropez (page 39)

7 Puerto Portals
Treat yourself to an evening at Tristan, the island's top restaurant (page 49)

8 La Trapa
This Trappist monastery, with its view over the rocky island of La Dragonera, is a popular spot (page 40)

is one of the most exclusive residential areas on Mallorca. Word has got around that Port d'Andratx, one of the few places where you can still see traditional fishing boats, is one of the most attractive ports in the Mediterranean, and consequently it has become a fairly expensive place to stay. The ★ promenade by the harbour, with its restaurants and boutiques, is very pretty and watching the sunset from here is an unforgettable experience. (A4)

HOTELS

Brismar
112 beds.
On the promenade; Category 2; Tel. 67 16 00

Villa Italia
An art nouveau villa which has been converted into a top-class hotel. Luxurious interior with marble baths, antique furniture, jacuzzis. Restaurant and terrace with a view over the harbour. 44 beds.
Port d'Andratx; Camino San Carlos 13; Category 1; Tel. 67 40 11

RESTAURANTS

El Patio
Best nouvelle cuisine, lovely atmosphere, charmingly lit inner courtyard.
Closed Tues and from Nov-Feb; Advance booking for evening only; Ctra. Andratx - Port d'Andratx; Category 1; Tel. 67 20 13

Rocamar
Excellent fish restaurant.
Closed Mon and from Dec-end of Jan; Advance booking essential; C/. Almirante Riera Alemany s/n; Category 1; Tel. 67 12 61

Villa Italia

Exquisite international cuisine, as you might expect from a hotel of this class.

Open daily; Advance booking essential; Camino San Carlos 13; Category 1; Tel. 67 40 11

SPORT

Club de Vela

Yachting marina with a great atmosphere and restaurant.
Tel: 67 14 34

SURROUNDING AREA

Sant Elm

Most westerly settlement on the island. Small sandy beach. Good base for hiking to the old Trappist monastery of ★ ⎝⎠ La Trapa. Worth the climb for the great view of Sa Dragonera island. (A4)

CALVIA

This unassuming town right in the middle of fertile cultivated land is said to be the richest in Spain. The district includes various resorts on the Costa de Calvià, from Portals Nous to Peguera. The modern town hall is a fine example of functional architecture and throughout the year exhibitions of avant-garde art works are held in the exhibition rooms. Entrance is free and the exhibitions can be viewed during normal working hours. (B4)

ILLETES

Charming resort very near Palma with both a rocky beach and a small sandy bay. The hotels here are some of the best on the island.

2 km to the south lies Bendinat, one of the more exclusive resorts on Mallorca. (B4)

HOTELS

Bonanza Playa

Health farm. 550 beds.
Ctra. de Illetes; Category 1; Tel. 40 11 12

Meliá de Mar

250 beds.
Paseo Illetes 7; Category 1; Tel. 40 25 11

RESTAURANT

Anchorage Club Bendinat

Superb international cuisine in wonderful surroundings.
Open daily (except Tues/Wed p.m); Advance booking essential; Category 1; Tel. 40 52 12

PEGUERA

Peguera lies on the road between Palma and Andratx so both holiday-makers and hoteliers are waiting impatiently for a by-pass to be built. Despite the through traffic, however, Peguera is a pleasant resort, popular both in summer and winter with longer-term residents. The town is ideally situated as a base for walks in the surrounding hills and the beach is only a stone's throw from the main road. There is a large supermarket on the road to Andratx (*open Mon-Sat 09.00-21.00 hrs, Sun 09.00-13.00 hrs*). (A4)

HOTELS

Beverly Playa

Direct access to beach. Nightclub. 800 beds.

Urb. La Romana; Category 2; Tel. 68 60 70

Cala Fornells I
Charming apartment complex with 85 units. Great views over the town and bay.
Category 2; Tel. 68 69 50

Villamil
Very popular establishment, though the rooms facing the road can be a bit noisy. 200 beds.
Ctra. Andratx; Category 1; Tel. 68 60 50

RESTAURANTS

La Gran Tortuga
❀ Breathtaking view of the sea from the terrace. International cuisine.
Closed Mon and Jan/Feb; Advance booking essential; Aldea Cala Fornells I; Category 1; Tel. 68 60 22

La Gritta
Italian cuisine, seafood specialities.
Closed 15 Nov-15 Jan; Advance booking essential in summer; Aldea Cala Fornells II; Category 1; Tel. 68 61 66

Rendezvous Garden
Mallorcan and international cuisine in this delightful palm-tree garden overlooking the sea.
Daily 10.00-02.00 hrs; Ctra. Andratx; Category 2

EVENING ENTERTAINMENT

Disco Palladium
Daily from Easter to October; C/. Gaviotas s/n

Rendezvous Dance Bar
For the over thirties.
Open daily all year; Ctra. Andratx

INFORMATION

Information Bus
Open Mon-Fri 09.00-13.00 and 14.30-17.00 hrs; Plaça Aparcaments; Tel. 68 70 83

SURROUNDING AREA

Es Capdellà
Charming village with attractive houses and gardens, 6 km north of Paguera. Good *café solo* in the Bar Nou. (A4)

Galilea
★ ❀ Mountain village 600 m above sea level with splendid views over the south-west coast. Snacks available in the Bar Parroquial next to the church. (B4)
(Closed Mon, Sat/Sun tapas)

PALMA

People still live in the old town, the *centre històric*, with its fine old buildings and magnificent houses, and the area is always busy and lively. The only way to explore the old town is on foot. It's not that big and it's great fun to meander along the streets and explore the alleyways. The old town is also a good place to indulge in some people-watching. When your feet begin to ache, sit and relax in one of the bars or cafeterias in the Plaça Major and watch the world go by. This square was formerly a medieval market-place and is situated at the upper end of the Borne.

The Borne (or more formally Passeig des Born) used to be the main street of Palma and the old tree-lined walkways with their stone benches still retain the elegance of bygone days. The historic coffee houses, once frequented by artists and writers, have been transformed into luxury boutiques, perfumeries and jewellers' shops. Their façades have recently been cleaned up and this facelift has given the whole street renewed sparkle. The Avenida Jaime III at the upper end of the Borne is a wonderful place for window shopping – in any weather! The walkways are covered over, providing protection from both sun and rain. From the lower end of the Borne, it's no distance to the sea and the Cathedral. This is where the real architectural gems of the city are to be found – the ★ *palacios*. Most of these magnificent houses are not open to the public, but a number of them, such as the Casa Oleo and the Casa Oleza in Calle Morey, do open their doors for a short period in the morning. These palatial mansions were modelled on Italian designs of the 15th and 16th centuries, when Palma enjoyed its heyday as a trading centre. Some of them are still owned by the descendants of these powerful merchants, while others have been modernized and turned into apartments.

The main shopping areas are squeezed into the streets around the Plaça Major such as Calle Sant Miquel, the Via Sindicato, the Calle Colón and the Calle Jaime II. There is an incredible mixture of exclusive boutiques and run-of-the-mill shops selling everyday items. The bars and restaurants are always busy, though the churches in this area seem to be attracting fewer people than they used to.

Amongst themselves, Mallorcans refer to Palma as the 'Ciutat'. This is a reference to its first name Civitas, which in Latin means city. The Romans also called the city Palmaria. The Moors, who settled on the island after the Romans, then translated *civitas* into *medina*, the Arab word for city. When the Christians replaced the Moors, the town was once again renamed and became Ciutat de Mallorca. It was not until the 16th century that the original name of Palmaria came back into official use in the shortened form of Palma.

Almudaina

This Arabic palace (*alcazar*) was once the royal home of the Kings of Aragon. It is used today by King Juan Carlos of Spain as his official residence whenever he

---

A holiday off the beaten track

The recently formed *Asociació de Agroturisme Balear* is an organization of about 40 country hotels and farms, offering holidays in the country to suit every taste and pocket. Ranging from 'basic' to 'very luxurious', the majority of these *fincas* are far from the major tourist areas and appeal primarily to those who are looking for peace and quiet in natural surroundings. For further information contact: Asociació de Agroturisme Balear, C/ Forners, 8, E-007006 Palma; Tel. 77 03 36, Fax. 46 69 10.

visits Mallorca. The 15th-century façade is a harmonious blend of Arabic and Christian architecture. This ancient palace boasts some splendid grounds known as S'Hort del Rei (the King's Garden). The courtyard, with its Gothic Chapel of Santa Ana, dates from the 13th century.

May-Sept 10.00-19.00 hrs, Oct-Apr 10.00-14.00 and 16.00-18.00 hrs; Closed Sat p.m./Sun; Guided tours only; Plaça Palau Real

Castillo Bellver

★ ⬥ The 'castle of the magnificent view' is a circular structure overlooking the city, with imposing walls and a light and spacious courtyard. The royal castle, which was completed during the reign of Jaime II in 1309, served as both fortress and gaol during the following centuries. The best time to visit is late afternoon when the light is at its best and the view over Palma is breathtaking. It can be approached from the El Terrano district and the road is well signposted. A recent addition to the castle's attractions is the Palma Historical Museum.

Daily 09.00 hrs until sunset

Cathedral (La Seo)

★ Palma Cathedral, also known as the 'Cathedral of Light', is considered to be one of the five most beautiful churches in all Spain. The central nave is 110 m long and is supported by 14 slim columns 20 m high. The large rosette in the apse dating from the 15th century and made up of 1236 pieces of stained glass, is more than 11 m in diameter. There is a wonderful view of the city and the harbour from the south portal, the Peutra del Mirador. It took more than 400 years to complete the Cathedral on the site of the former main mosque. The foundation stone was laid on New Year's Day, 1230, by King Jaime I after the capitulation of the Arabs, and the last section of the main portal was completed in 1604, nearly 400 years later. The entrance is through a side door on the north side of the building and leads directly to the chapter house where the Cathedral treasure is on display.

Daily except Sun and public holidays, 10.00-17.30 hrs in summer and 10.00-14.00 hrs in winter; Sat (all year) 10.00-14.00 hrs; Plaça Palau Real

Cloister of San Francisco

This cloister boasts the largest Gothic quadrangle in Europe. It is probably also the noisiest as it is used by the cloister school pupils as a playground. The Franciscan cloister was founded in 1232 on the site of an Arabic mosque. The first recorded description of the church dates from 1281 – a single-nave Gothic long hall with marbled side chapels. Behind the main altar lies the grave of the saintly Raimundus Lullus (see p.18) and there is a bronze memorial to Fray Junípero Serra (see p.18) in front of the church.

Lonja (La Llonja)

The old Maritime Exchange in Palma, built between 1426 and 1451, is one of the masterpieces designed by the architect Guillermo Sagrera. It is a vast building, with numerous windows and an elegant interior which features six spiral columns. Today, La Llonja is one of the most prominent forums for art exhibitions. Information about current exhibitions and opening hours can be obtained from the tourist information office.

Miró Centre and Museum

★ The artist Joan Miró (1893-1983) lived and worked on Mallorca for 40 years and bequeathed a great many of his paintings to the city of Palma on his death. Around 100 of them, some unfinished, are on display in this museum. The Miró Centre also puts on exhibitions of works by internationally renowned contemporary artists.
Daily (except Mon) 11.00-18.00 hrs, Sun 11.00-14.00 hrs; C/. Saridakis 30/31; Calamajor; Tel. 40 58 58

Museo de Mallorca

There are some 3000 items on display in the museum which is housed in the 17th-century Palacio Ayamans. All the major periods of Mallorcan history are covered – prehistoric, classical, medieval, Renaissance and Baroque. The Gothic portraits from the 14th and 15th centuries are of particular interest, as are the archaeological finds from the Roman settlement of Pollentia which are laid out in the basement rooms.
Daily (except Mon) 10.00-14.00 and 16.00-19.00 hrs, closed Sun p.m.; C/. La Portela 5

Museo Diocesano

This museum has a good collection of ceramics, coins and prayer books along with fine examples of Gothic painting dating from the 14th and 15th centuries.
Daily (except Sun) 10.00-13.00 and 15.00-18.00 hrs; C/. Mirador (at the south portal of the Cathedral)

SHOPPING

Alpargatería La Concepció
Alpargatas (linen shoes with hemp soles).
C/. Concepció 17

Casa Bonet
Lace and embroidery.
C/. Puidorfila 3

Charles Jourdan
Quality shoes at reasonable prices.
Avda. Jaime III, 12

Licorería Llofriu
Original Mallorcan herbal liqueurs, *palo (aperitivo), hierbas (digestivo)*, genuine *sobrasada, butifarra* and Mallorcan hams.
C/. San Nicolás 22

HOTELS

Arabella Golf Hotel
Health farm. Tennis courts, golf.
Urb. Son Vida; Category 1; Tel. 79 99 99

Borne
Renovated *palacio*. 100 beds.
C/. San Jaime 3; Category 3; Tel. 71 29 42

Melía Victoria
On the Paseo Marítimo. 335 rooms.
Avda. Joan Miró 21; Category 1; Tel. 73 25 42

Palladium
106 beds
Paseo Mallorca 40; Category 2; Tel. 71 39 45

San Lorenzo
12 beds. Cosy and comfortable city hotel.

The grand Casa Belloto in Palma

C/. San Lorenzo 6; Category 2; Tel. 72 82 00

Son Vida
Large luxury hotel with golf course. 340 beds.
Urb. Son Vida (5 km outside the city); Category 1; Tel. 79 00 00

RESTAURANTS

Bahía del Mediterráneo
Exquisite restaurant located on the 5th floor of the Edificio Mediterráneo. Exceptional seafood and nouvelle cuisine. View over the bay. Very much the current 'in' place.
Daily (except Sun); Advance booking essential; Paseo Marítimo 33; Category 1; Tel. 28 25 07

Koldo Royo
Spanish masterchef Koldo Royo opened this restaurant in 1989, specializing in Basque dishes and nouvelle cuisine.
Closed Sat p.m./Sun; Advance booking essential; Paseo Marítimo 3; Category 1; Tel. 73 24 35

La Lubina
Specializes in fresh seafood. Terrace open in summer. Own parking facilities.
Open daily; Advance booking essential; Muelle Viejo (on the harbour); Category 1; Tel. 72 33 50

El Parlament
Mallorcan cuisine of the highest order, *paella* a speciality. This restaurant allows you to order paella for just one person, which is fairly unusual. Popular lunchtime rendez-vous with politicians.
Daily (except Sun); C/. Conquistador 11 (in old Parliament building); Category 2; Tel. 72 60 26

Sa Premsa
✪ Large Mallorcan restaurant in a converted garage where diners are seated on wooden benches. There is no advance booking and sometimes you have to queue to get in.
Mon-Fri; Plaça Bisbe Berenguer i Palau (also known as Plaza de los Patines); Category 3

Club de Mar

Yachting marina near the city. 610 berths. Disco. Good service.
Paseo Marítimo; Tel. 71 87 83

Real Club Náutico

Well-established yachting marina with pleasant atmosphere. 890 berths, restaurant, hotel, shops.
Paseo Marítimo; Tel. 72 68 48

Son Vida Club de Golf

18-hole course.
Urb. Son Vida; Tel. 79 12 10

ENTERTAINMENT

Bar Abaco

The most original bar in Palma, located in a 17th-century palace. Excellent cocktails. Décor includes abundance of fresh flowers and candles. Classical music.
Daily from 21.00 hrs; C/. San Juan 1

Bar Barcelona

♣ Unpretentious. Good atmosphere. Live Latin-American music from 23.00 hrs.
Daily from 22.00 hrs; C/. Apuntadores corner of C/. San Juan

Bar Bosch

Bar with terrace open all day. The whole of Palma seems to congregate here in the evening.
Daily (except Sun) 07.00–03.00 hrs; Plaça del Rei Joan Carles

La Bóveda

Bar, restaurant, music venue and pub rolled into one. The district around Llonja has become the trendy place to be in Palma, with lots of bars and lively atmosphere.
Daily, midday and evenings; Carrer Sa Portería 2

Tito's Palace

♣ Great disco with a view of the bay by night. 6 bars and room for 2000 clubbers. Entrance on the Plaça Gomila.
Daily from 23.00 hrs, in winter-weekends only

Victoria

Piano bar for the fashion conscious. Varied choice in music ranging from golden oldies to the latest hits.
Daily from 22.00 hrs; Paseo Marítimo, beneath the Hotel Meliá Victoria

INFORMATION

Avda. Jaime III 10; Tel. 71 22 16
Plaça d'Espanya; Tel. 71 15 27
C/. Santo Domingo; Tel. 72 40 90
All offices open daily except Sun, 09.00–14.30 and 15.00–20.00 hrs, Sat 09.00–13.30 hrs

SURROUNDING AREA

Gènova

Village on the slopes of the Sierra Na Burguesa above Palma. It can be reached from Sant Agustí or from the Palma-Peguera motorway. The route is well signposted. Lots of typically Mallorcan bars, where you can get good food for very reasonable prices. One of the bars which deserves a special mention is Gonzalo I. It has a ❀ barbecue and terrace in summer and is popular with Mallorcan families. (B4)
Daily (except Thurs); Category 3

Pórtol and Sa Cabaneta

The two main ceramic centres (see p.29) are situated 15 km north-east of Palma – with workshops and showrooms. (C4)
Can Bernadí Nou. Sa Cabaneta,

C/. Jaime I 6; No telephone. Toni Serra, Pórtol, C/. Roca Llisa 1; Tel. 60 20 89

PALMANOVA/ MAGALUF

These neighbouring resorts have developed and expanded to such an extent over the last few years that they are now adjoining and practically one giant resort. However, there is a marked contrast between the two. In Palmanova, on the one hand, are 13 of Mallorca's 60 four-star hotels, a casino with floor show and the largest disco in Europe. Magaluf, on the other hand, is the prime destination for cut-price holidays. These cheap package deals draw many a 'lager lout' intent on having a riotous holiday. Some of the more unscrupulous bar owners don't exactly discourage the drunk and disorderly. Only concerned with making a fast buck, they offer lethal cocktails and put on 'drinking contests' that don't always end happily. And yet, just beyond the high-rise apartment blocks lies a completely different world. Nearby Cala Figuera boasts a gentle rural landscape of fields and woods. This attractive and peaceful bay lies at the end of a lovely 15-km drive south along the picturesque Palma-Peguera road. (B5)

HOTELS

Punta Negra
Situated on a headland, this hotel also has adjoining bungalows. 120 beds.
Ctra. Andratx; Category 1; Tel. 68 07 62

Son Caliu
Well-run hotel with health farm, far from the madding crowd. 450 beds.
Palmanova, Urb. Son Caliu; Category 1; Tel. 68 23 00

SPORT

Aquapark
Aquatic fun and games for all ages.
Daily 10.00-17.00 hrs; Closed 1 Nov-1 May; Ctra. Magaluf-Cala Figuera; Tel. 13 08 11

Club Náutico Palmanova
Basic marina. 70 berths.
Tel. 68 10 34

Dive with Nemo
'Nemo' dives several times a day to depths of 40 m.
Nemo-Centre, Magaluf; Avda. Magaluf 18; Tel. 13 02 27

Golf de Poniente
18-hole course.
Ctra. Cala Figuera s/n; Tel. 13 01 48

Port Adriano
Yachting marina between Magaluf and Santa Ponça. 466 berths.
Urb. El Toro; Tel. 10 25 65

ENTERTAINMENT

BCM Disco
✝ Europe's largest disco, 5 bars, 460 000 watt sound-system, 12 500 watt light-show, laser show, video clips, pool, spectacular beauty contests and pop-stars.
Daily 22.00-05.00 hrs; Magaluf

Casino de Mallorca
One-armed bandits, black-jack, roulette and floor show. Passport essential.

Daily 20.00-04.00 hrs; Magaluf; Tel.
13 00 00

PLAYA DE PALMA

The so-called 'naked mile' starts 9 km south-east of Palma Cathedral and stretches for 5 km along the coast. Immediately behind the beach there is a promenade partially lined with palm trees. On the opposite side to the beach there are rows of bars, shops, cafés and hotels. The beach is divided into 9 sections marked out by *balnearios*, or beach huts. The motorway from Palma runs parallel to the beach and there are three exits – at Can Pastilla (Balneario 2), Las Maravillas (Balneario 5) and in S'Arenal (Balneario 8). The more upmarket hotels are concentrated around Balnearios 4 and 5 and they are open all year round. This is where the RIU-Centre, the meeting point and heart of the Playa de Palma, is located. The 'naked mile' is international and liberal in outlook and topless bathing is perfectly acceptable. (C4)

HOTELS

Gran Bahía
450 beds.
S'Arenal, C/. Bartolomé Calafell s/n;
Category 3; Tel. 26 13 90

Río Bravo
200 m from the beach. 400 beds.
C/. Misión de San Diego s/n; Category 1; Tel. 26 63 00

San Francisco
Well-established hotel on the Playa de Palma. 275 beds.
C/. Laud 24; Category 2; Tel. 26 46 50

RESTAURANTS

Bodega Oliver
Fish and meat dishes.
Daily; Can Pastilla, C/. Albatros 11;
Category 2

Rancho Picadero
Mallorcan cuisine. Lamb is a speciality.
Daily; Can Pastilla C/. Flamenco;
Category 2

SPORT

Club Marítimo San Antonio
Yachting marina with 390 berths. Restaurant.
Can Pastilla; Tel. 26 35 12

Club Náutico
Yachting marina with 630 berths. Restaurant.
S'Arenal nr Balneario 9; Tel. 26 89 85

Windsurfing
The Bay of Palma is an ideal spot for windsurfing fanatics, thanks to the gentle south-westerly winds which average between force 4 and 5. You can hire a board at Balneario 9 at the Club Náutico, and for beginners there are windsurfing schools at Balnearios 3 and 7.

ENTERTAINMENT

Hofbräuhaus Latino
German café with Latin American music and dancing.

Oberbayern
Disco with plenty of atmosphere.
Daily; Between Balnearios 6 and 7

RIU-Palace
✝ Enormous disco in the RIU-Centre with 4 bars and a laser

show. Maximum capacity 4000!
Daily; Balneario 5.

PORTALS NOUS

This area consists of several built-up zones with villas, holiday homes and apartments set in the hills behind the Palma-Andratx road. (B4)

RESTAURANT

Tristan
★ The top restaurant on Mallorca, serving exquisite nouvelle cuisine. Very high standard, with prices to match.
Daily during summer months, evenings only (Bistro open for lunch with a more reasonably priced menu). Daily during winter months (except Mon) Closed 15 Nov-15 Dec; Advance booking essential; Puerto Portals harbour; Category 1; Tel. 67 55 47

SPORT

Marineland
Amusement park and marine biology centre with dolphin shows and a chance to dive for pearls. Cafeteria.
Daily 09.30-18.45 hrs; Closed 20 Nov-24 Dec; Portals Nous-Palma road; Tel. 67 51 25

Puerto Portals
Said to be the best yachting marina in the Balearics. King Juan Carlos has been known to berth here. 640 berths.
Tel. 67 63 00

SANTA PONÇA

Santa Ponça is made up of three distinct areas – the medieval *finca*

which gave the settlement its name, the area around the harbour where most of the villas are situated, and the modern holiday resort with its hotels, apartments and all the hustle and bustle you would expect. There are a lot of foreigners who have second homes here and English is widely spoken. (A5)

HOTELS

Club Galatzó
Good hotel for sporty people in a quiet location. Tennis courts, golf course. Bus to Palma and the beach. 380 beds.
Approach from Palma-Peguera motorway; Category 1; Tel. 68 62 70

Golf Santa Ponça
Hotel-Residencia close to the golf course. 36 beds.
Category 1; Tel. 69 02 11

RESTAURANT

El Ceibo
Latin-American grill restaurant.
Daily (except Mon), evening only; Closed 20 Dec-1 Mar.; C/. Ramón Montcada, Edificio Xaloc; Category 2

SPORT

Club Náutico Santa Ponça
Sheltered marina. 520 berths.
Tel. 69 30 58

Golf Santa Ponça
18-hole course.
Urb. Santa Ponça; Tel. 69 02 11

INFORMATION

Tourist Information Office
C/. Puig de Galatzó s/n; Tel. 69 17 12

Wild mountains, spectacular coasts

Hair-pin bends and breathtaking views along Mallorca's picture-book coastline

The drive along the coast road that winds its way over the cliff tops from Banyalbufar via Sóller to Sa Calobra is an exhilarating experience that you're unlikely to forget in a hurry. The mountainous landscape is stark, wild and breathtakingly beautiful. The sea glistens far below, while inland the imposing mountains of the Serra del Nord tower above you. (The two highest mountains on the island are Puig Major at 1445 m, and Puig Massanella at 1349 m.) On rounding each bend, a fantastic panorama opens out in front of you.

Much of this thinly populated part of the island is given over to terraced fields and olive groves. The irrigation systems adopted here can be traced back to Moorish times, particularly those in use around Banyalbufar and the Sóller valley. Fresh spring water seems to bubble up everywhere. The ancient olive groves around Valldemossa and Deià are im-

Valldemossa is one of the most popular destinations, with around 150 000 visitors to the Carthusian monastery each year

pressive and even a little eerie. Some of the trees are over 300 years old, their trunks gnarled and twisted with age.

To get to the secluded rocky bays, you need to follow the hair-raising, narrow and winding roads which rise and fall steeply for miles and miles. The only sandy beach of any significant size along this stretch is at Port de Sóller. The south-eastern slopes of the Serra del Nord are most densely populated in the area around Inca, and this is where almond and fruit orchards as well as vineyards are cultivated.

Small manufacturing industries and handicraft businesses have benefited from the road which cuts diagonally across Mallorca, and the Palma-Inca railway line, both of which have opened up this area to tourists. However remote and cut off from the coast some of the towns and villages in this region may appear, none of them is further than 40 km from the sea.

BANYALBUFAR

This small town at the foot of the 926-m high Puig d'Esclop is dependent on its almonds and cereal crops for survival. The vineyards that gave the town its name ('Bany-al-bahr' is Arabic for 'vineyard by the sea') have largely been replaced by crops such as tomatoes, grown on the artificial terraces, first laid down by the Moors. Banyalbufar is a popular base for exploring the surrounding mountainous countryside. (A3)

SHOPPING

Good selection of ceramics and pottery in the shop directly opposite the parish church.

HOTELS

La Baronia
75 beds.
C/. General Goded 13; Category 3; Tel. 61 81 46

Marivent
40 beds.
C/. José Antonio 49; Category 3; Tel. 61 80 00

SURROUNDING AREA

Atalaya de Ses Animes
Watchtower dating from the 16th century, now used as a viewing platform, 3 km west of Banyalbufar. (A3)
Daily, no charge.

Estellencs
Picturesque mountain village, starting point for the ascent of Puig de Galatzó (1026 m). Narrow bay. Old Mallorcan restaurant Es Grau, which has magnificent views from its terrace, situated nearby. (A4)
Daily, lunch only; Andratx-Estellencs road; Category 2

La Granja
★ Feudal complex of Arabian origin boasting a magnificent garden with fountains. The main building dates from the 17th century. A traditional 'Mallorcan Feast' with folk dancing is held here on Wednesdays and Fridays. It is only possible to visit the castle as part of a

MARCO POLO SELECTION: NORTH-WEST

1 Son Alfabia
The gardens are a magnificent example of Moorish landscaping (page 56)

2 La Granja
A fine blend of Moorish architecture and Mallorcan rural tradition (page 52)

3 From the Monastery at Lluc to Sa Calobra
Dramatic views along a breathtaking island road (page 57)

4 Fornalutx
Mallorca's most picturesque village (page 57)

5 Valldemossa
Carthusian monastery and birthplace of the island's patron saint (page 58)

6 La Residencia at Deià
Hotel built in the style of a medieval villa (page 53)

7 Son Marroig
Archduke Ludwig Salvator's former residence (page 59)

guided tour. (B3-4)
Daily 10.00-19.00 hrs; Banyalbufar-Esporles road; Entrance 1300 ptas; Tel. 61 00 32

Mirador Ricardo Roca

◢◣ Viewing platform built in 1913 by the Mallorcan Tourist Board. (A4)

DEIÀ

The 'artist village', as it is referred to, is perched on top of a hill at the foot of Puig Teix (1026 m). One quarter of its 400 inhabitants are 'expats' who have been drawn to the village because of its beauty and atmosphere, as well as its history. Prominent artistic and literary figures once gathered here. The poet and author Robert Graves had a home here from the 1930s until his death in 1985 (see p.19). The main street snakes upwards from the lower village to the former Arabic arsenal where the church and graveyard are located. Deià is a quiet, pleasant village and is never crowded, even during the peak season. Tourist buses are not permitted to stop here, and there is a sleepy air about the place. But this doesn't mean that nothing ever happens here. Classical concerts featuring internationally renowned musicians are frequently held, both here and in the neighbouring village of Son Marroig. The gastronomic offerings are incredible considering the size of the village. Nowhere else in Mallorca has such a high concentration of good-quality restaurants, and the two four-star hotels here are among the best on the island (which means they are booked up well in advance). (B3)

SIGHTS

Church and Graveyard

The parish church of San Juan Bautista, whose tower was originally designed for military rather than spiritual purposes, boasts a statue of Christ that dates back to Roman times. Robert Graves, best known for his historical novel about the Emperor Claudius (see p.19), is buried here. He died in 1985 at the age of 90. Another grave, that of the German artist Ulrich Leman, shows that he was 102 years old when he died. There must be something about Deià that promotes long life!

SHOPPING

The best bread you'll ever taste can be found in the high street bakery. It also sells newspapers.

HOTELS

Es Molí

Absolute perfection. The surroundings are wonderful, the garden magnificent and the service discreet but efficient. The hotel serves lemon and orange juice freshly squeezed from fruit picked in the gardens. Paradise. 145 beds.
Category 1; Tel. 63 90 00

La Residencia

★ In an old country mansion on the outskirts of the village on the road to Sóller. 54 beds.
Category 1; Tel. 63 90 11

RESTAURANTS

Can Jaume

Rustic, Mallorcan cuisine.

Hotel La Residencia, Deiá

Daily (except Mon), Sat evenings only in Jan/Feb; Main street; Category 2

Christians Bar
Bar and restaurant with a limited menu. Popular with the locals. Terrace.
Daily; Main street; Category 3

El Olivo
Very stylish restaurant in a converted olive oil mill. Serves some of the best nouvelle cuisine on the island.
Daily, evenings only during the summer; Closed Feb; Advance booking essential; Near the Hotel Residencia; Category 1; Tel. 63 93 92

Suizo
International cuisine with an emphasis on Swiss specialities.
Daily, evenings only except Tues; Advance booking essential; Main street; Category 1; Tel. 63 91 39

EVENING ENTERTAINMENT

Bar Las Palmeras
The terrace overlooking the main street tends to be taken up by lo-cals. A place where people go to see and be seen – but prices are reasonable.

SURROUNDING AREA

Llucalcari
The smallest village on the island with only 11 inhabitants, Llucalcari lies on the road between Deià and Sóller about 1.5 km from the former. The tiny, rocky beach can be reached only on foot. The water is crystal clear. The Costa d'Or hotel (84 beds, *Category 3; Tel. 63 90 25*) is here. (B3)

INCA

With 20 000 inhabitants, Inca is Mallorca's third largest town. It lies inland, half-way along the road from Palma to Alcúdia in the north. The narrow, twisting streets are a legacy of the Moorish settlers and the church of Santa María la Mayor, with its magnificent bell tower, was built on the site of the former mosque. The church is open only during services.

Inca is a lively market town where you'll find traders and craftsmen, light industry and agriculture. There is a market every Thursday, and as it's the centre for the leather industry, you'll see plenty of leather goods for sale. Take a good look around before you buy anything though, as prices and quality tend to vary. There are plenty of good restaurants and Inca is famous for its *celleres* which are converted wine cellars, with huge vats and wooden tables where you choose from traditional dishes listed on hand-written menus.(C3)

Asinca
Leather clothes.
C/. Salord 26; Tel. 50 12 50

Yanko
Shoes.
On the C-713, shortly before entering the town coming from Palma

Celler Can Amer
Meat and stews.
Daily (except Sat/Sun); C/. Pau 39; Category 2; Tel. 50 12 61

Celler Can Ripoll
Traditional Mallorcan cuisine.
Daily (except Sun and Sat evening during winter); C/. Jaume Armengol 4; Category 2; Tel. 50 00 24

Celler Molí Vell
Very spacious. Traditional Mallorcan cuisine.
Daily (except Mon); Avda. Bisbe Llompart, 38; Category 2; Tel. 50 00 46

Aqualandia
Aquatic theme park.
Daily 09.00-17.30 hrs; Adults 750 ptas, children 400 ptas; On the C-713, 25 km, Foro de Mallorca

Castillo de Alaró
Ruined fortress above Alaró with a snack-bar restaurant and accommodation. Turn off at 'Es Pouet' sign, 3 km from Alaró on the road to Orient. Footpath opposite the Hotel L'Hermitage. Fantastic view. (C3)

Lluc Monastery
The most important pilgrimage site for Mallorcans since medieval times. In the church, where the Moreneta, the Madonna of the Mountains, is honoured, a choir of children from the music school give a daily concert at 11.15 a.m. (except during school holidays of course). There are two bar-restaurants in the grounds of the monastery and a large souvenir shop. The small museum displays everyday objects and musical instruments spanning the previous three centuries, as well as prehistoric finds from some of the excavations on the island. There is also a collection of paintings by the Catalan artist Coll Bardolet. The most spectacular route on the island starts here and ends in Sa Calobra. (C2)
Daily 10.00-17.30 hrs; Entrance 200 ptas; Approach from Inca road via Selva and Caimari

Orient
This quiet village, with only 30 inhabitants, lies in splendid isolation on the road from Alaró to Bunyola. Unembellished stone houses, a number of which have been bought and restored by foreigners, surround the church. If you have the time, it's worth stopping here for lunch to sample the local speciality. This is a delicious pork and apple dish, of which the villagers are justifiably proud. Or you could even spend the night here in the island's most authentic country hotel. L'Hermitage has tennis courts, a swimming pool, horse-riding and good international cuisine. 40 beds. (C3)
Ctra. Sollerich, 8 km; Category 1; Tel. 61 33 00

Puig d'Inca

Inca's local mountain lies about 4 km east of the town. You can go on an excursion to the now deserted Hermitage of Santa Magdalena which was built right up on the mountainside. There are picnic areas with great views. The whole district has been designated a nature reserve, but there is one Mallorcan restaurant offering good, basic food. (D3)
Daily (except Tues)

Son Alfabia

★ The gardens are a magnificent example of Arabic pre-eminence in garden design. The vegetation is lush and it's very pleasant, almost therapeutic, to listen to the softly tinkling water. The Moorish governor of Inca, Benihabet, who converted to Christianity in 1229, was responsible for the layout of these gardens. The 17th-century house, built in the baroque style, is now a museum. (B3)
Daily 09.30-19.00 hrs; Entrance 500 ptas; Palma-Soller road, 17 km

Very close to the gardens is the Ses Porxeres restaurant which serves extremely good Catalan food.
Daily (except Sun evenings and Mon); Closed Aug; Advance booking essential; Category 1; Tel. 61 37 62

SÓLLER/ PORT DE SÓLLER

A wonderfully romantic tram, dating from 1912, connects the town of Sóller with the Port de Sóller about 5 km away. Both town and port lie in a sunny valley, ringed by the mountain ranges of the Serra d'Alfabia, L'Ofre and Puig Major. Citrus fruits are cultivated in the valley. The regularly abundant harvests are largely a result of the excellent irrigation system introduced by the Arabs, which is still in use. The Arabs settled in the 'Golden Mussel' (Arabic *suliar*) around AD 950. Port de Sóller has become a popular resort, and fishing boats and yachts now berth where merchant ships, which brought such wealth to the region, once anchored. The harbour walls are now used as parking spaces for tour buses and cars.

The best way to reach Sóller from Palma is to use the railway line – first opened in 1912 and electrified in 1927 – which connects both places. There is a service that runs five times a day. The 'Red Lightning' train takes about 50 minutes to complete the journey from the station in the Plaça d'Espanya in Palma to

---

In the Marco Polo Spirit

Marco Polo was the first true world traveller. He travelled with peaceful intentions, forging links between the East and the West. His aim was to discover the world, and explore different cultures and environments without changing or disrupting them. He is an excellent role model for the 20th-century tourist. Wherever we travel we should show respect for other civilizations and the natural world.

WWF

Sóller. If you want to go by car, there are two routes you can follow – the C-711, which includes 65 sharp bends as it winds its way over the 496-m high Coll de Sóller, or the C-710, the coastal route from Andratx or Pollença. In 1994, a tunnel was built through the Serra d'Alfabia, running parallel with the railway, which meant that there was a direct road at last. (B2-3)

SIGHTS

Museo Etnológico
The Ethnological Museum in the Casa de Cultura has a display of furniture, ceramics and everyday objects from the 18th and 19th centuries.
Daily (except Sun/Mon), 10.00-14.00 and 15.30-17.30 hrs; Voluntary contribution of 150 ptas recommended; C/. de Mar 5

SHOPPING

Daily covered market and a flea-market on Saturdays.

HOTEL

Espléndido
Hotel on the promenade. Service is excellent. 208 beds.
Open Apr-Oct; Marina Es Traves 23; Category 2; Tel. 63 18 50

RESTAURANTS

Es Canyis
Best Mallorcan cuisine. Seafood specialities.
Daily (except Mon) Mar-Oct; Port de Sóller, Platja den Repic s/n; Category 2

El Guía
Good, basic Mallorcan food.

Daily; closed Mon in winter; C/. Castaner 1 (in station); Category 3

SPORT

Puerto de Sóller
Marina located in the harbour. 136 berths.
Tel. 63 16 99

SURROUNDING AREA

Fornalutx
★ The village of Fornalutx is perched above the Port de Sóller. The majestic Puig Major, the highest mountain on the island, rises up in the distance and provides a wonderful backdrop. This idyllic setting has twice earned Fornalutx the title of the 'most beautiful village in Spain'. You get a great view over the valley from the ☙ terrace of the Bar Bellavista. It takes about one hour to walk from here to Sóller via Biniaratx. (C3)

Sa Calobra
This is one of the most visited spots on the island. It can be reached by boat from Port de Sóller or by ★ road which

The picturesque mountain village of Fornalutx

The Torrent de Pareis - a spectacular backdrop for swimmers

branches off from the C-710 between Sóller and the monastery at Lluc. The road that takes you down to the coast twists and turns, rises and falls over 800 m, before reaching the secluded village of Sa Calobra by the sea. The village itself is nothing to write home about – there isn't much here apart from a couple of souvenir shops, a hostel and a handful of modest restaurants. But the scenery is something else. Two 200-m high rock tunnels lead to a tiny cove, where the Torrent de Pareis, an amazing canyon some 4 km long, opens out into the sea. During the winter months this canyon is filled with the sound and fury of stormy waters racing to the sea. During the summer, the surrounding area provides some of the best hiking country on the island. (C2)

VALLDEMOSSA

★ This village, set in a fertile valley (411 m above sea-level), owes its fame and popularity to the fact that the composer Frédéric Chopin and his lover, the French writer George Sand, spent a few weeks together, during the legendary 'wet winter' of 1838/39, in the recently secularized Carthusian monastery (see p.59). More than 150 000 visitors a year come to the area on the strength of their names alone. But Valldemossa is a place of beauty in its own right. The streets around the birthplace of Santa Catalina Tomás are a blaze of colour thanks to the profusion of flowers in the area. (B3)

SIGHTS

Carthusian Monastery

The present-day buildings of the medieval monastery date from the 18th century. These include the pharmacy, a wonderful building in its own right. The cells, formerly used by the monks, have a garden which affords a lovely view over the valley. This was where Chopin and George Sand spent the winter of 1838/39. Every year, a festival celebrating the music of Chopin is held here in July and August. There is a printing press that dates from the 15th century. The best times to visit are in the morning before 10.30 or during the afternoon.

Daily (except Sun) 09.30-13.30 and 15.00-18.00 hrs; Entrance 900 ptas

HOTELS

Can Marió

Plain and simple, but very beautiful. 16 beds.

C/. Wetam 8; Category 3; Tel. 61 21 22

Vistamar

Stylish hotel in a former country house. Good restaurant. 18 beds.
2 km along the C-170 in the direction of Banyalbufar; Category 1; Tel. 61 23 00

RESTAURANTS

Can Pedro

Mallorcan cuisine.
C/. Archiduque Luis Salvator; Daily (except Sun evenings and Mon); lunch only during winter; Category 2

Can Costa

Excellent Mallorcan cuisine.
Daily (except Tues); lunch only during winter; 3 km along the C-710 in the direction of Deià; Category 2

INFORMATION

In Valldemossa town hall.

SURROUNDING AREA

Port de Valldemossa

A 6-km twisting and narrow road with great views leads to the port. The rocky beach is flanked by steep cliffs. (B3)

Son Marroig

★ The country residence of Archduke Ludwig Salvator of Austria (see p.13), is situated halfway between Valldemossa and Deià. The house, which has been made into a museum, features furniture, paintings, books, photographs and other objects connected with the Archduke. There is a fabulous view of the countryside from the marble temple in the garden.
Daily, 10.30-14.00 and 16.30-18.00 hrs; Entrance 250 ptas
〰️ The Son Marroig restaurant beneath the house offers good Mallorcan cuisine and a great view out over the sea. (B3)
Daily (except Mon); Category 3

Els Ermitans

〰️ This settlement, with its spectacular location above the coast, was founded in 1648 by the monk Juan Mir Vallés from Alaró. It is the centre for the Hermitage of Saints Paul and Anthony. (B3)
1.5 km along approach road, opposite Can Costa restaurant

Around Cap Formentor

Rich in history and rugged beauty, with the largest reserve of marshland in the Mediterranean

The north-east coast is dominated by two wide bays – the Bay of Pollença and the Bay of Alcúdia. They are separated by the mountainous peninsula of La Victoria, which juts out 6 km into the sea. The Bay of Pollença is rocky and largely made up of numerous tiny coves. The Bay of Alcúdia has wider stretches of sandy beach that are more accessible and appealing to holiday-makers. To the east of Can Picafort, the coastline becomes rocky again, dotted with more cliffs and small coves. The mountains of Artà provide a spectacular backdrop to these coves or *calas*. A number of them, like Cala Mesquida for example, have been developed to attract more tourists.

If you want to go for a scenic mountain drive, take either the road from Artà to Can Picafort or the one from Artà to Betlém. The mountain road that leads from Port de Pollença to the northernmost point of Cap Formentor is particularly spectacular.

Follow in the footsteps of the Romans at the excavations at Pollentia near Alcúdia

The ★ Albufera Gran is the largest area of marshland in the Mediterranean. It lies in the Alcúdia/Sa Pobla/Muro triangle and was officially designated a nature reserve in 1988. A number of canals criss-cross this area which covers 17 000 hectares. The marsh is separated from the beach at Bahía de Alcúdia by a wide sandbank. The terrain is a naturalist's dream, with its lush vegetation and extremely varied wildlife. It's a breeding ground for all types of fish and amphibians and there are over 200 species of birds.

Inland, the Albufera Gran borders on the rich farmland of Sa Pobla and Muro. These fertile fields were once marshland too, but the area was drained over a century ago so that it could be used for cultivation.

Most of the hotels in the resorts are closed between mid-October and mid-April, but in towns like Pollença, Alcúdia and Artà the shops and restaurants generally stay open for business throughout the year. This is a great place to come in winter if you're looking for absolute peace and quiet.

ALCÚDIA/PORT D'ALCÚDIA

This pretty country town lies between the Bays of Alcúdia and Pollença. It is completely enclosed by medieval walls. The church of San Jaime was built into one of the corners of the walls and there are two magnificent gates made from yellow sandstone – the Puerta de San Sebastián opens out to the south, in the direction of Palma, and the older Puerta de Xara opens out towards the port. If you walk right round the ancient city walls, you'll come across a small bull-fighting arena, which is at least 100 years old. As you might expect, the town is compact, and the streets are narrow and provide plenty of shade. There are a number of ancient buildings and the town hall takes pride of place among them. The streets, which rise up gently to the centre of the town, were laid out by the Arab settlers. When they landed in the Bay of Alcúdia in 903, they came across the ruins of the Roman town of Pollentia, which had been destroyed by Vandals in around 450. Instead of building on top of these ruins, the Moors decided to found a new settlement on the hill which led down to the sea, which was how Alcúdia got its name (*al-kudia* means 'on the hill' in Arabic). They made this settlement the new capital of the island. In time, Palma became more important but the rivalry between Alcúdia and Palma is still strongly felt today. The power station at Alcúdia has supplied Mallorca with its electricity for more than 60 years now and also provides the power for the neighbouring island of Menorca.

Alcúdia's own tourist empire stretches out on both sides of the La Victoria peninsula. The Bay of Pollença has been almost completely developed and you'll find the smaller resorts of Mal Pas and Bonaire here.

In the Bay of Alcúdia, however, there are still a few places that the developers haven't managed to get their hands on yet. The most important resort along this stretch of coast is Port d'Alcúdia, which is about 3 km south

MARCO POLO SELECTION: NORTH-EAST

1 Nuestra Señora de la Victoria
Drive or walk from Alcúdia to the Church of 'Our Lady of Victory', then on to Atalaya d'Alcúdia for a wonderful view (page 65)

2 Formentor Peninsula
Take a trip to Cape Formentor and swim at Cala Pí de la Posada (page 71)

3 Albufera Gran
Spend a day in the wilderness of this nature reserve, just beyond the beach at Alcúdia (page 61)

4 International Music Festival at Pollença
Chamber music and solo performances in the former Santo Domingo Monastery (page 69)

One of the two fortified gates in Alcúdia

of the town itself. This is the liveliest fishing port and marina on the north-east coast of the island. In summer it is usually jam-packed with tourists who fill the large hotels and apartment complexes. Entertainment is generally confined to discos and the numerous bars. (D-E2)

SIGHTS

Excavations on the site of the Roman town of Pollentia

These Roman ruins lie directly on the road to Port d'Alcúdia, alongside the church of San Jaime.
Daily from sunrise to sunset

Museu Monográfic de Pollentia

This is where the finds from the excavations at Pollentia are kept - masonry, shards of pottery and coins. There are also models of reconstructed Roman houses on display.
Daily (except Mon) 10.00-13.00 and 15.00-18.00 hrs; C/. San Jaime 2

Teatro Romano

All that remains of the Roman theatre are the foundation walls, but it's still a very impressive sight. The signpost which stands at the 51-km point on the road from Alcúdia to Port d'Alcúdia is weatherbeaten and can be easily missed, so keep a sharp eye out. The site itself is about 200 m off the main road.

Church of San Jaime

The current church building dates from the 16th century, though the original church foundations date even further back to around 1248. The interior is designed in Spanish Gothic style and has two impressive stone pulpits and an attractive main altar. The chapel is baroque, and is home to the Santo Cristo crucifix, which is paraded on 26 July, the feast of St Anna. You can ask for the key to the church at the presbytery, (*Casa Rectoral*).

SHOPPING

Weekly market in the town on Sundays.

HOTELS

Alcúdia Park

Modern hotel near the beach. 650 beds.
Ctra. Alcúdia-Artá, 5 km; Category 2; Tel. 89 05 56

Bahía de Alcúdia

Family hotel near the beach. Aviary. 470 beds.
Avda. de la Playa; Category 2; Tel. 54 58 00

Mal Pas

Family-run hotel in the Mal Pas district. 180 beds.
Playa Mal Pas; Category 3; Tel. 54 51 43

Royal Fortuna Playa
In the Playa de Muro district. 420 beds.
Ctra. Alcúdia-Can Picafort; Category 2; Tel. 89 03 22

RESTAURANTS

Aucanada Club
Good Mallorcan cuisine.
Daily (except Mon); Port d'Alcúdia, Urb. Aucanada; Category 2

Casa Parco
International cuisine.
Daily; Alcúdia harbour road; Category 2

Miramar
Excellent fish restaurant.
Daily (closed 1 Dec-15 Jan); Advance booking essential; C/. Vicealmirante Moreno 4; Category 1; Tel. 54 52 93

SPORT

Because the Bay of Pollença is such a sheltered location, it is an ideal place for beginners to learn water-sports (windsurfing, water-skiing, sailing).

The same can be said for the Bay of Alcúdia, but be warned, a north-westerly wind can spring up suddenly and perhaps carry the unwary out to sea. You can hire windsurfing equipment in Port d'Alcúdia.

Puerto Deportivo Alcúdia
Large harbour with 728 berths. Diesel can be obtained in the neighbouring fishing harbour.
Tel. 54 60 00

El Cocodrilo de Bonaire
Smallish marina in Mal Pas with 335 berths.
Tel. 54 69 55

Happy Sailing Española
School for sailing and windsurfing. Yachts also available for chartering.
Open end of April-mid November; Alcúdia, Carrer de la Mata 1; Tel. 54 71 29

Nuevas Palmeras
Sports centre at the Sunwing Hotel. Good for tennis.

Hidro Park
Swimming pool with water-chutes, suitable for children and adults.
Daily 10.00-19.00 hrs, closed Nov-May; Port d'Alcúdia, Avda. Tucán s/n; Tel. 89 16 72

ENTERTAINMENT

Wide choice of pubs, discotheques and bars catering for all tastes and budgets.

SURROUNDING AREA

Campanet
This rural village is on the Alcúdia-Palma road at the foot of Puig Tomir (1103 m). The church of Sant Miquel is one of the oldest churches on the island. Built around 1220, it was recognized as a Christian place of worship even during the Arab occupation. The caves (Cuevas de Campanet) are the smallest on Mallorca but are generally considered to be the best. The tour of the caves takes only about 20 minutes, but it's fascinating. Just at the turn-off from the C-713 to Campanet, you'll find the glass factory and museum of La Menestralía. There is a weekly market set up in the main street on Tuesdays. (D2)

Nuestra Señora de la Victoria

★ ◁◁ If you head 100 m south of Puerta de Xara in Alcúdia, you'll come across a sign directing you to the 'Ermita de la Victoria'. This is a pilgrimage church built high up on the peninsula of La Victoria. To get to the sanctuary of 'Our Lady of Victory' you have to travel for about 2.5 km along a quiet road, which is more suitable for walking than driving. Turkish pirates stole the small figure of the Virgin from the chapel in 1551. Legend has it that the figure was miraculously found back in her original place the very next day. Seven years later, the Turks made a second attempt at stealing the statue, but the miracle was repeated. This miracle finally persuaded the Turks to give up their attempts to take Alcúdia.

The view from the church terrace is remarkable, but there is an even better view from Atalaya d'Alcúdia, which can be reached after a one-hour hike. The view encompasses both the Bay of Pollença and the Bay of Alcúdia, with the stark mountains of Cabo Farrutx in the east. There's a good restaurant if you're in need of sustenance after the climb. (E2)

Mirador de la Victoria; Daily (except Mon); Ctra. Cabo Pinar, Ermita turnoff; Category 2

ARTÀ

At first sight, Artà (pop. 5700) is not a welcoming town. If you approach from the south, the first thing to catch your eye is the imposing fortified church, over which the ramparts of the castle stand guard. Even the railway station at the foot of the hill doesn't look terribly friendly – grey walls surround the terminus. It was opened in 1875 for the railway line that used to run right across the island from Palma, via Inca to Manacor and Artà. Once you enter the town itself, however, the picture changes for the better. The road leading to the town hall slopes gently upwards past attractive houses, whose strong walls are softened by the abundant displays of flowers that hang from them. When you reach the fortified church, consecrated in 1248, you get a great view of the surrounding area. The present church of the Transfiguración del Señor, was built during the 16th century. Behind the church there is a lovely wide flight of steps flanked on either side by cypress trees. These steps lead to the pilgrimage church of San Salvador on top of Calvary Hill. Again, the view over the town is breathtaking. The yellow, red and grey rooftops make a pretty picture. You'll have realized by now that first impressions can be deceptive and that Artà really is a very attractive place indeed. Even the castle, the former Arabic *alkazar,* later home to Mallorcan royalty, looks much less forbidding from here. The golden walls are lit up by the sun and the sound of cascading water can be heard from the courtyard. There are trees that provide welcome shade and the whole place is very inviting. It is a perfect spot in which to relax and enjoy some peace and quiet.

The name of the town originates from the Arabic *jertan,* meaning garden, and it's obvious where it gets this name from. The town is surrounded by fertile orchards and rich farmland, which has served all the town's needs since medieval times. This natural wealth attracted pirates from North Africa and Turkey, and Artà had to learn to defend itself against invaders. This explains the presence of the rather ugly defensive walls that dominate the town. One of the largest Bronze-Age sites on Mallorca, Ses Paisses, can be found in the nearby fields around Artà. (F3)

SIGHTS

Castillo

The castle was originally built by the Arabs and later became home to the kings of Mallorca. Well worth a visit.
Daily, 10.00-18.00 hrs

Museo

The town museum is in the same building as the bank. It displays the finds from the Bronze-Age *talayot* settlement (see p.17), along with various other objects dating back to Phoenician, Greek and Roman times.
Mon-Fri, 10.00-12.00 hrs; C/. Rafael Blanes 8

Ses Paisses

Massive Cyclopean walls beneath ancient olive trees dominate the site of this *talayot* settlement. The huge entrance gate is still in relatively good repair and the outlines of the various buildings can be seen quite clearly. An extensive complex, which you can freely explore, has been designated as a 'Royal Palace'. Unfortunately, the excavations have come to a halt and there is no indication when, or even if, they will start again. You can visit the site at any time.

SHOPPING

Weekly market in the town on Tuesdays.

RESTAURANT

Can Faro

Basic but substantial Mallorcan cuisine.
Daily (except Fri evenings and Sat lunchtime); On the street from the station to the town hall; Category 3

SURROUNDING AREA

Ermita de Betlém

For over 9 km, an attractive route leads you first of all through some gentle countryside to the fortress-like buildings of Son Morey Vell, then the road begins to climb, twisting and turning over the pass between Puig de Sa Font Crutis and Puig de Sa Palmera until it descends again down to the settlement in the valley. The first settlers here had to spend their first night in a stall – hence the name Betlém, or Bethlehem.

There are parking spaces in front of the main gate. If you follow the sign saying 'Fuente', you come to a grotto with a statue of the Virgin Mary. There is another sign behind the church, which is not usually open to visitors, directing you to a 'Mirador', or view point. You can get a fantastic view from here that spans the entire Bay of Alcúdia and you can see as far as the La Victoria peninsula. From the top of the watchtower, even higher up, you can see the Colònia de Sant Père which lies on the rocky coast. This little fishing village has recently become a popular resort. (E 2-3)

CAN PICAFORT

Once an old fishing village, Can Picafort is today a busy resort, which is usually heaving with tourists in summer. It is basically a one-street town – admittedly, this street is nearly 3 km long. The main thoroughfare is called Avenida Reina Sofía and is lined with bar after bar, pub after pub and shop after shop. The hotels, which mushroomed in the 1960s, are mostly in the lower-price category and are particularly popular with young people and families with young children. During the winter, however, it empties out and becomes a real ghost town.

Can Picafort got its name from a lumberjack called Jeroni Fuster who put up the first house there. His nickname was 'Picafort' ('Give it a whack!'). With a name like that, he deserved to have a town named after him! (E2)

SIGHTS

Necropolis Son Real

Immediately beyond the last houses of the Son Bauló district, the excavations of the largest necropolis ever found in Spain are on view. Graves of every shape – oval, rectangular, square and round – stand out eerily against the sand dunes. These graves date back over one and a half thousand years! They cover the periods from the late Bronze Age and the early Phoenicians during the first millennium BC, right through to the Roman period in the first century BC. On excavation, most of the graves were found to contain between two and six skeletons, and they were all facing east. Jewellery and other everyday utensils were also found, which helped archaeologists to date them. Unfortunately, the locals have tended to use the site as a bit of a dumping ground, so watch out for that Bronze-Age tin of beans! The site can be visited at any time.

SHOPPING

Weekly market is in town on Tuesdays (from June to September only).

HOTELS

Can Picafort

Right on the beach. 200 beds.
Via Alemania s/n / Avda. Cervantes s/n; Category 3; Tel. 85 01 09

Clumba Mar

In a side street, 250 m from the beach. 470 beds.
C/. Arenal 24; Category 2; Tel. 85 00 01

Farrutx

Near the centre, 200 m from the beach. 320 beds.
Avda. Trías s/n; Category 3; Tel. 85 00 11

Gran Vista

600 m from the centre and beach. 554 beds.
Ctra. Alcúdia-Artá; Category 2; Tel. 85 00 52

RESTAURANTS

Juan Mandilego

Exquisite seafood restaurant.
Daily (except Mon); Closed 15 Dec-30 Jan; Advance booking advisable; C/. Isabel Garau 49; Category 1; Tel. 85 00 89

Quick service for tourists

It's a common myth that tourists are always in a hurry and leave themselves little time to eat. That's why some restaurants have perfected this so-called 'quick service'. This means that no sooner have you finished one course than your plate is whisked away and the next appears. If you prefer to eat your meal at a more leisurely pace, don't order the main course until you've finished the starter. It might annoy the waiter, but it means you'll eat in peace.

Los Patos

Large restaurant with children's play area. Basic Mallorcan cuisine, good service.
Daily (except Tues); At the turn-off to Muro on the Can Picafort-Alcúdia road; Category 2; Tel. 89 02 65

INFORMATION

Tourist Information Office

Plaça Ingenerio Gabriel Roca 6; Tel. 85 03 10

SURROUNDING AREA

Muro

This ordinary Mallorcan town is only about 5 km inland from the resort of Playa de Muro, and the neighbouring Can Picafort. The *Museo Etnológico,* the Ethnological Museum, is worth seeing. It is housed in a typical Mallorcan town residence, and the displays on two floors give a good idea of what life was like for the average Mallorcan citizen during the 18th and 19th centuries. (D3)
Daily (except Mon) 10.00-14.00 and 16.00-19.00 hrs; C/. Major 5

SPORT

Puerto Deportivo

Yachting marina with 473 berths, maximum length 12 m, fresh water supply.
Tel. 85 00 10

Rancho Andaluz

Riding centre and base for pony trekking.

Rojo Vivo

Sports centre with good tennis facilities in the Son Bauló district.

Sport Pins

Tennis courts at the Gran Vista Hotel.

ENTERTAINMENT

Gabriel

Bar with dance floor, international clientele.
Ctra. Artà 25
When 'Gabriel' closes, the many other discos open their doors and stay open until the early hours.

Sa Pobla

❧ The centre of the Mallorcan fruit and vegetable industry, Sa Pobla doesn't have all that much in the way of interesting sights or museums. But if you happen to be in Mallorca on 17 January, there is a parade that takes place known as the '*Revetla de Sant Antoni*' (see p. 33) – St Anthony's day and the traditional procession enacting the driving out of the devil is quite a colourful event. So is the gathering of artists on the last Sunday of November, the 'Trobada dels pintors', when hundreds of artists, both professionals and enthusiastic amateurs, meet to exhibit their work. (D2)

POLLENÇA/ PORT DE POLLENÇA

This modest town (pop. 10 000) lies inland in the shadow of the Puig de Ternelles. The first settlers were refugees from Alcúdia who fled here to escape the continual pirate raids of the 14th century. They gave their new settlement the name of the ancient Roman capital, Pollentia, which had occupied the site where Alcúdia now stands. In 1552, however, they suffered another pirate raid during which the new settlement of Pollença was razed to the ground. So it wasn't until the 16th century that the town really began to take shape. The townspeople set about rebuilding their homes immediately after this attack, and the result is a pleasant little town made up of narrow, shady streets, which have something of the feel of an Arab *medina* about them. It is a very unpretentious place, even the churches are modestly built. The present building of the church of Santa María de los Angeles, first consecrated in 1236, dates from the 18th century and is quite spartan in style. There is also an old Jesuit church, Montesión, dating from 1697, which stands next to the town hall. You can climb the hill of Puig de Calvari (170 m) via the flight of 365 steps that starts behind the Plaça Major. From the top, standing beside the small Neo-Gothic chapel, you get a view of both the town and the fertile plains which lie beyond the Torrent San Jordí. The old Roman bridge spanning this gorge is the only example of Roman architecture on the island that remains intact (see p.70).

A number of internationally renowned musicians are drawn to the town by the concerts which take place during the ★ International Music Festival, held in the former Dominican monastery of Santo Domingo. They come both as performers and spectators. The area around Pollença is also very popular with foreigners who want to take up permanent or semi-permanent residence on Mallorca. Many of the old *fincas* (country estates) have been transformed into luxurious villas with swimming pools and all mod cons. All this only serves to confirm what one Mallorcan businessman said around the turn of the century – 'Pollença is the place where all the really refined people go'. He could have included Port de Pollença in this statement. This resort is only 5 km away from the main town. The port is no longer a working fishing harbour and there is now a small and exclusive marina instead. The conditions for sailing here are hard to beat. (D1-2)

SIGHTS

Santo Domingo
Cloister and courtyard were built in 1578. A statue of the Madonna is the focal point of the religious festival celebrated on the Monday preceding Ash Wednesday.
Daily 09.00-18.00 hrs; On the right as you leave the town

Roman Bridge

This solidly-built stone bridge with two arches spans the Sant-Jordí river, which is nearly always dry. It has lasted well over 2000 years. Living proof of Roman engineering skills.

To the north of the town

SHOPPING

Galería Bennássar

Exhibits contemporary art, mostly Mallorcan.

Plaça Major 6; Tel. 53 35 14

Galerías Vicens

Hand-woven textiles, with Mallorcan *llengua* (tongue) motif, in various forms and colours.

On the road to Port de Pollença s/n

HOTEL

Illa d'Or

Old establishment, furnished in traditional Mallorcan style. 240 beds.

C/. Colón s/n; Category 2; Tel. 86 51 00

RESTAURANTS

Daus

Good Mallorcan cuisine with an imaginative touch. Specialities include rabbit with lobster and partridge with cabbage and apricots.

Daily (except Tues); Closed last week Nov-last week Jan; Escalonada Calvari 10; Category 2; Tel. 53 28 67

La Lonja del Pescado

Seafood restaurant with a great view over the harbour.

Daily (except Wed) Closed Jan/Feb; Port de Pollença, Dique Muelle s/n; Category 1; Tel. 53 00 23

SPORT

Club Náutico Port de Pollença

Yachting marina with 375 berths, maximum boat length 30 m. Restaurant.

Tel. 86 46 35

Golf Pollença

9-hole course with clubhouse, driving range and professional coach.

Ctra. Palma-Pollença, 49.3 km; Tel. 53 32 16

Sail & Surf school

Basic instruction and examination for beginners. Tips on fast and efficient sailing for more advanced sailors. Yacht and boat charter available.

Port de Pollença, Playa de la Gola; Tel. 86 53 46

INFORMATION

Tourist Information Office

Port de Pollença, C/. Miquel Capllonch s/n; Tel. 53 46 66

SURROUNDING AREA

Cala Sant Vicenç

This former fishing village on the north coast, 8.5 km from Port de Pollença, is an exquisite resort with a narrow beach between imposing cliffs. There are a number of prehistoric caves nearby. The walk to Punta de Covas takes about 30 minutes and the views are simply breathtaking. (D1)

Castillo del Rey

A 9-km trail leads through the mountain country of Ternelles to the coast. The few remaining supporters of the Mallorcan King, Jaime III, made a desperate last stand, after his defeat by Pedro IV of Aragón, here in the 'King's Castle'. You have to obtain a permit for the trail from the Banca March in Pollença. (D1)

Formentor Peninsula

★ ٭ The Formentor peninsula, with its wild 400-m high cliffs, juts out 13 km into the sea. Some of the more remote coves and bays, like Cala Figuera, can be reached only by boat. The best base from which to explore this untamed region is Port de Pollença. You can also take the boat from here to Cala Pí de la Posada, still considered to be the best beach on the island. At one time it was reserved for the exclusive use of guests staying at the Hotel Formentor, but now it is open to all. The Hotel Formentor, opened in 1929, is a very traditional establishment. The hotel register has included a number of illustrious names over the years. The location is extremely peaceful. There is a large garden and formal dress is expected in the dining room. 240 beds. (D-E1)
Playa de Formentor; Category 1; Tel. 86 53 00

Puig de María

٭ If you're brave enough (and have a small manoeuvrable car), try the ascent to the summit of the 330-m high mountain and the village of Mare de Déu del Puig. The last stretch is on foot and a bit steep. The climb requires some effort, but your reward is a tremendous view. (D2)

Stunning view of Cap Formentor at the northern tip of the peninsula

Coast of a hundred bays

Hidden inlets and sandy coves

The eastern part of the island, from Cala Ratjada in the north to Cabo de Ses Salines and Colónia de Sant Jordí in the south, has some of the most diverse and varied countryside on Mallorca. The coastline stretches for some 80 km with countless coves and bays *(calas)* cutting into it along its entire length. Standard maps show about a hundred of these inlets, while the more detailed nautical charts reveal that there are more than double that number. This area of coastline can be roughly divided into three sections. The largest *cala* is a broad sandy bay called Cala Millor/Cala Bona which lies in the northern section. The central section, known as Calas de Mallorca, is made up of a series of 20 or so smaller *calas* which dominate the rocky landscape. The smallest, most intimate bays, like Cala S'Aumonia and Cala Figuereta, are found in the southern section. They are often no more than 20 m wide

Cala Figuera, the former harbour of Santanyi, has become a popular resort for young people in the last 30 years or so

and are tucked in between the steep cliff faces. The only way to gain access to these secluded little beaches is from the sea.

Running parallel with the coast about 2-5 km back from the sea is the road from Cala Ratjada to Colónia de Sant Jordí. There are a number of minor roads branching off it at intervals which lead directly to some of the bays along this coast. To the west, the Serra de Levante rises to a height of 509 m and the monastery of San Salvador near Felanitz is perched on this summit. The further south you go, the more varied the landscape becomes. Long dry-stone walls enclose well-tended fields, white *fincas* stand out in stark contrast against the green of the fruit orchards, and bright geraniums and bougainvilleas mingle with the opuntia cactus – more familiarly known as prickly pears. This is one of the most fertile regions on the whole island, hence the name S'Horta or Cala d'Or (*hort* is the Mallorcan word for garden and Cala d'Or is derived from Cala d'Hort). The principle towns in this region are Manacor and Felanitx.

MARCO POLO SELECTION: EAST AND SOUTH-EAST

1 Villa Sa Torre Cega
Open-air museum of contemporary art in Cala Ratjada (page 77)

2 Portocolom
Every house in this old fishing village has its own private jetty (page 81)

3 Coves del Drac
Stalactite cave near Portocristo with an amazing underground lake (page 81)

4 Cala Mondragó
This peaceful bay near Portopetro is one of the loveliest on the east coast (page 77)

5 Botanicactus
Europe's largest botanical garden has around 40 000 species of flora (page 80)

6 Castell de Santueri
Ruined fortress to the south of Felanitx with a spectacular view of the east coast (page 80)

CALA FIGUERA

The old harbour of Cala Figuera, which has become a popular resort with young holiday-makers, lies at the mouth of the Torrent dels Oms, as it emerges from a steep gorge, guarded by a 16th-century watchtower. Cala Figuera is now a major international resort and has a good selection of small, reasonably priced hotels and *pensiones* (guesthouses) above the harbour. It is a lovely spot with an atmosphere all of its own. (E5)

HOTELS

Cala Figuera
200 beds.
C/. Tomarimar 30; Category 3; Tel. 64 52 51

Villa Sirena
Very popular *pension*. 90 beds.
C/. Virgen del Carmen 37; Category 3; Tel. 64 53 03

SPORT

Octopus
Diving school near the harbour.

ENTERTAINMENT

Moon Bar
⚓ Popular meeting place with entertainment laid on.
C/. Virgen del Carmen

SURROUNDING AREA

Cala de Santanyi/Cala Llombards
Narrow bays with about 60 m of sandy beach, to the south of Cala Figuera. The Hostal Playa (18 beds, Category 3) is located right on the beach. Four other bays - Cala Sa Comuna, Cala S'Aumonia, Cala Figuereta, Cala Marmols - can be reached by boat from Cala Figuera. (E5-6)

Santanyi
This town (pop. 7000) seems to be able to carry on with its every-

day business unaffected by tourism. The majority of houses here are made from the golden-yellow sandstone quarried in the vicinity of Santanyi. This stone was also used in the construction of a number of medieval buildings in Palma.

One of the most precious organs in the whole of Spain, designed and built by Jordi Bosch, can be seen in the church of Sant Andrés Apóstol. The key to the church is available in the presbytery, the Casa de la Rectoría, opposite. (E5)

CALA MILLOR/
CALA BONA

If you want to cross over to the Cala Millor (literally the 'better' bay) from the adjoining Cala Bona (the 'good' bay), then you only have to stroll across a narrow bit of land that connects them. These two bays have been discovered by the tourist industry and have experienced a real boom in recent years. A holiday resort, especially geared towards families, gradually developed here over the years between 1960 and 1990, and today it is the second largest tourist centre on the island. The hotels here fall mainly into Category 3. The beaches are free from all traffic and the *mini-tren*, a miniature railway, is the most popular way of getting about. The train also connects the area with the towns of Son Servera and Sant Llorenç. To the north of Cala Millor/Cala Bona lie the elegant settlement of Sa Costa des Pins and the resort of Canyamel in a secluded bay. To the south are Sa Coma, Cala

Moreya, S'Illot and Cala Morlanda – small bays that stand out against a dark background of fragrant pine trees. (F3)

HOTELS

Can Cruia
Five-star *finca* right by the sea.
Canyamel; Category 1; Tel. 58 59 11

Eurotel Punta Rotja
Hotel with golf-course. 460 beds.
Sa Costa des Pins; Category 1; Tel. 56 76 00

Granja S'Heretat
Country hotel.
Capdepera-Canyamel road; Category 2; Tel. 81 83 99

Royal Mediterráneo
Large hotel complex on the beach. 780 beds.
Sa Coma; Category 1; Tel. 81 01 05

SPORT

Club de Golf de Son Servera
9-hole course.
Urb. Sa Costa des Pins; Tel. 56 78 02

Puerto Cala Bona
Small yachting marina with 136 berths. Maximum boat length 8 m. Diesel. Drinking water.
No telephone

Tennis Center
Cala Millor, just off the main road

ENTERTAINMENT

Bar Pacha's
⚓ Music and dancing under the stars, popular with the young crowd.
Daily; Beach road, at the Hotel Don Juan

Q
Glass palace next to the Hotel Said. Disco, beer garden.
Daily

Steffany's
⚲ One of the top discos.
Daily; Main street

Tourist Information Office
Daily, 09.00-13.00 and 15.00-19.00 hrs, in winter 09.00-14.00 hrs; Parc de la Mar 2; Tel. 58 54 09

Reserva Africana
There are 500 animals from the African continent living in this large wild-life park. Car essential. (F3-4)
Cala Millor-Portocristo road; Daily 09.00-18.00 hrs, in winter until 17.00 hrs; Tel. 81 09 09

Son Servera
Pretty town at the foot of Puig de Sa Font. On Sunday mornings in the Bar Nuevo there is a substantial tapas buffet. (F3)

CALA D'OR/
PORTOPETRO

The small rocky cove of Cala d'Or is a lively place in summer, with a charming beach for swimming and sunbathing, and a number of boutiques, bars and terrace cafés. Portopetro lies in the neighbouring bay 1.5 km to the south. This fishing village has only 250 inhabitants and is home to Club Méditerranée on Mallorca. There are several bars and restaurants. (E5)

Cala Esmeralda
302 beds.
Urb. Cala Esmeralda; Category 1; Tel. 65 71 11

Club Cala Barca
2300 beds. Family holidays in the pine woods.
Portopetro; Category 2; Tel. 64 35 34

Gran Hotel Tucán
310 beds.
Bulevard s/n; Category 1; Tel. 65 72 00

Can Trompe
International and Mallorcan cuisine.
Daily (except Tues in summer); Avda. Bélgica 4; Category 2

Es Clos
Nouvelle cuisine specialities.
As you come into Alquería Blanca on the road from Santanyi; Category 1; Tel. 65 34 04

Villa Roca Serena
Rustic grillroom.
Daily in summer; In the bungalow complex at Cala Serena, Ctra. Cala Serena; Category 2

Club Hípico Cala d'Or
Sailing, riding, mini-golf, bowling. Restaurant.
Daily; Avda. Portopetro; Tel. 65 70 04

Rancho Bonanza
Pony-trekking and dressage.
Daily, May-Oct; Urb. Cala Egos; Tel. 65 73 37

a Morena Diving Center

Diving school at Cala Gran (Cala d'Or).

Vall d'Or Club de Golf

18-hole course.
Ctra. Cala d'Or-Portocolom, 7.7 km; Tel. 83 70 68

Marina Cala d'Or

Sheltered marina, 435 berths. Restaurant, shop, no fuel.
Tel. 65 70 70

Real Club Náutico

Very well maintained marina in Portopetro. 228 berths.
Tel. 65 76 57

SURROUNDING AREA

Santuari de la Consolació

Sanctuary of St Scholastica, the 'rainmaker'. A quiet spot with a small church. The road from Alquería Blanca is well signposted. (E5)

Cala Mondragó

★ This double bay is a beautiful spot, with clean, clear water and very few buildings. Nature reserve since 1990. (E5)

CALA RATJADA

Cala Ratjada is a popular place with the younger crowd. It has many regulars and is also popular with young families who enjoy the friendly atmosphere of the basic, one-star hotels, of which there are plenty. Cala Ratjada is good value for money and very lively. Water sports are big here - you can windsurf, sail and dive. If you prefer sports on dry land, there are tennis facilities for all levels. You can even get lessons from the resident coach. A *mini-tren* links the two beaches of Cala Angulla and Son Moll, a 15 minute walk from the old town centre. (F3)

SIGHTS

Villa Sa Torre Cega

★ This villa, on a hill overlooking the harbour, is owned by the wealthy March banking family. It has an open-air museum of contemporary art set in the extensive grounds. There is an emphasis on modern Catalan sculpture.
Tel. 56 30 33

HOTELS

Bella Playa

On the beach at Cala Guya. 430 beds.
Avda. Cala Guya 125; Category 2; Tel. 56 30 50

Pino Mar

Small comfortable hotel.
Category 2; Tel. 56 40 13

Es Vinyet

170 beds.
C/. Mateo y Catalina 1; Category 3; Tel. 56 55 51

RESTAURANTS

S'Hera de Pula

Renowned restaurant. Mallorcan and international cuisine.
Daily (except Mon); Closed 10 Jan-30 Mar; Advance booking essential; Ctra. Capdepera-Son Servera; Category 1; Tel. 56 79 40

Es Molí

Excellent Mallorcan cuisine.
Daily; Ctra. Capdepera, 1 km; Category 2

The Cala Guya at Cala Ratjada - a dream of a beach

Ses Rotges
Finest French cuisine.
Daily; Closed 1 Nov-30 April; Advance booking essential; C/. Alsedo s/n; Category 1; Tel. 56 31 08

SPORT

Mero Diving School
Free snorkelling between 12.00-13.00 hrs, May-Oct.
Cala Lliteras; Tel. 56 54 67

Puerto Deportivo
Small yachting marina, only basic facilities available. Fresh water supply. No fuel. Maximum length 12 m.
Tel. 56 40 19

Windsurfing club Font de Sa Cala
Training courses. Boards and boats for hire.
Tel. 56 44 36

ENTERTAINMENT

Bolero
Live music and disco.
Daily in summer; Town centre

Robert
International bar on main street.
Daily, April-Oct

Xiroi
♰ Disco with pool.
Daily, weekends only in winter; Son Moll Hotel Gili

INFORMATION

Tourist Information Office
Daily (except Sat p.m. and Sun) 11.00-13.30 and 16.00-19.00 hrs; Plaça dels Pins s/n; Tel. 56 30 33

SURROUNDING AREA

Cala Mesquida
Wild and beautiful sandy bay 3 km north of Cala Ratjada. (F2)

Capdepera
The 14th-century castle, which is reached by climbing the steep set of steps from the Plaça de Orient, is the largest on the island. (F3)
Daily, in summer 10.00-13.00 and 16.00-19.00 hrs, in winter 10.00-13.00 and 15.00-17.00 hrs.
There is also a market here on Wednesdays.

Coves d'Artà
Caves beneath Cabo Vermell whose walls have been blackened by smoke. The entrance is reached by climbing a rugged set

of steps, cut into the rocks for a visit by the Spanish Queen, Isabella II, 150 years ago.
Daily, 10.00-19.00 hrs in summer, 10.00-17.00 hrs in winter

CALAS DE MALLORCA

This is the name given to the 20 or so small bays and coves between Portocolom and Portocristo. Most of them are accessible only from the sea, but a few like Calas Magraner, Virgili, Bota, Soldat, Setri and Antena have tracks leading down to them. There are six modern hotels in this area with a total of 3200 beds. The complex is attractively laid out. The built-up area above Cala Murada is not really worth visiting. (E-F 4-5)

RESTAURANTS

El Gran Mesón
Fine restaurant specializing in seafood.
Daily; Playa Romántica, C/. Amapola 48; Category 2; Tel. 82 06 26

SURROUNDING AREA

Hidden Bays
The best way to explore the charming coastline of this part of Mallorca is by boat. A nautical chart has at least twice the number of coves and bays shown on a normal map. The boat trip from Cala Murada to Portocristo makes for a wonderful day out.

COLÒNIA DE SANT JORDÍ

There are countless numbers of bars and restaurants crammed together around the harbour in this small port (pop. 3000). The hotels and holiday apartments have been built on the outskirts. Colónia de Sant Jordí is blessed with wonderful beaches which don't get overcrowded even during high season. Es Trenc, a beautiful stretch of coastline which runs for about 5 km, is now a protected area while the beaches of Els Dolç and Ses Roquetes to the south provide another 3 km of unspoilt coast. This is one of the quieter, less crowded resorts on the island. (D6)

HOTELS

Marqués de Palmer
422 beds.
Colónia de Sant Jordí s/n; Category 2; Tel. 65 51 00

Romántica
482 beds.
C/. Carabela s/n; Category 3; Tel. 65 53 50

RESTAURANTS

Lonja del Pescado
Seafood restaurant by the harbour wall.
Daily; weekends and public holidays only in winter; Category 2

Es Trenc
Restaurant on the beach of Es Trenc offering international cuisine.
Daily in summer; Category 2

SPORT

Caballo Negro
Riding school for children and beginners.
Estanques centre s/n; Tel. 65 50 55

Puerto Deportivo
Basic marina with 370 berths. Maximum depth, 0.9 m. No fuel. Restaurant.
Tel. 65 51 48

Bedais Water Sports Centre
Diving, windsurfing and sailing.

SURROUNDING AREA

Botanicactus
★ The largest botanical garden in Europe (15 hectares) with over 40 000 plant species. Many varieties of cacti. Artificial lake. (D5)
Daily 09.00-20.00 hrs; just outside Ses Salines on road to Satanyi

Ses Salines
Quiet rural town (pop. 3000) with fortress-like houses. Market every Thursday. (D 5-6)

FELANITX

This town (pop. 14 000) is the centre of the *azulejos* (blue tile) industry, and the export centre for Mallorca's 'green pearls', the exquisite capers. A market is held every Sunday in the market hall by the town hall, and the 50-strong town band holds frequent open-air concerts. (E5)

SIGHTS

Sant Miquel
This charming 18th-century parish church, first consecrated in 1248, has an impressive flight of steps leading up to the entrance.

HOTELS

Sa Posada d'Aumallia
Magnificent country mansion. The 14 rooms may be furnished with antiques, but this hotel has all the comforts you would expect from modern accommodation. Swimming pool, tennis courts, horse-riding.
Camino Son Prohens 1027; Category 1; Tel. 58 26 57

RESTAURANTS

Vistahermosa
Mallorcan and international cuisine in a rural setting. Swimming pool and tennis courts.
Daily; Closed 20 Nov-end of March; Ctra. Felanitx-Portocolom 6 km; Category 1; Tel. 82 49 60

SURROUNDING AREA

Castell de Santueri
★ ☀ Ruins of an Arabic fortress built on Roman foundations, 440 m above sea-level. Excellent view. Key is held in the Sa Possesció des Castell manor house on the approach road. (E5)
Daily; Branch off from the C-714, 3km out of Felanitx on the way to Santanyi

Santuario de San Salvador
☀ Monastery set on a hill 509 m above sea-level. The present building dates from 1716 and the church has an impressive painting of the Last Supper dating from around 1500. The crib *(belén)* is well worth seeing. (E5)
Daily 09.00 hrs-sunset; Approach road 4 km from the PM-401 from Felanitx (well signposted)

MANACOR

The 'metropolis of the east', Manacor (pop. 25 000) is Mallorca's second largest town. Manacor is very much a working town, with not a great deal in the way of tourist attractions. There aren't many hotels, because although hundreds of people visit Manacor every day, they tend to come on day trips to visit the pearl factories or to have a look around one of the 60 or so workshops that produce many of Mallorca's souvenirs. The pearl factories turn out around 50 million artificial pearls per annum. (E4)

SHOPPING

Cerámicas y Decorativos
Souvenirs of all kinds.
Daily; Ctra. C-715, km 48; Tel. 55 14 07

Oliv-art
Woodwork.
Daily; Ctra. C-715, km 47; Tel. 55 02 30

Perlas Majórica S.A.
Artificial pearls.
Shop Mon-Fri 09.00-13.00 and 14.30-19.00 hrs, a.m. only on Sat/Sun. Factory tour available Mon-Fri; Via Roma s/n; Tel. 55 09 00

PORTOCOLOM

★ This unspoilt fishing village (pop. 1800) is the old port of Felanitx. The harbour is almost totally enclosed and every house on the waterfront has its own landing stage. The hotels and holiday apartments are concentrated outside the village itself around the large bay. The little beaches can be reached by car or on foot. (E5)

RESTAURANTS

Molí d'en Sopa
Good Mallorcan cuisine.
Daily; Closed 15-30 Jan; Ctra.

Manacor-Portocristo, km 4; Category 2; Tel. 55 01 93

Sa Sinia
Good seafood restaurant by the harbour.
Daily (except Mon); C/. Pescadores s/n; Category 2

SPORT

Club Náutico
Charming marina with 250 berths. Maximum depth 3 m.
Tel. 82 46 58

Poseidon Diving School
Courses in diving, windsurfing and sailing at the Hotel Vistamar.

PORTOCRISTO

The former harbour of Manacor (pop. 2400), 13 km inland, is a busy, lively resort during the summer months. (F4)

SIGHTS

Coves del Drac
★ Inside these caves, first explored by the French speleologist Edouard Martel in 1896, lies the island's largest underground lake, Lago Martel (177 m long, 40 m wide and 9 m deep). Fantastic stalactite formations.
Daily Apr-Oct, 10.00-17.00 hrs, Nov-Mar limited access for one hour only at 10.45, 12.00 and 14.00 hrs. Concert at 15.30 hrs; Tel. 82 07 53

SPORT

Club Náutico
Basic marina in sheltered location with 400 berths. Fuel. Maximum length 19 m. Restaurant.
Tel. 82 08 80

The fertile plain

*Discovering the island's agricultural heart,
rich farmland since Roman times*

The large plain of Mallorca, Es Plá, spans the island from the borders of the north-west coastal region down to the south-west coast, and stretches from the Serra del Nord in the west, with its 40 1000-m peaks, to the Serra de Levante in the east. The plain itself is not completely flat. There are some hills that rise up out of it, such as Puig de Randa with its three monasteries, lying between Llucmajor and Algaida, Bonany to the south of Petra, with the sanctuary to the Virgin Mary named after the hill itself, and the monastery on Montesión near Porreres.

Es Plá de Mallorca is rich farming country where a wide variety of crops are cultivated. In the north-east, in the area around Sa Pobla and Muro, vegetables and fruit are the principal crops, while in the south-west, near Llucmajor and Porreres, almonds and apricots are the major produce.

The market in the ancient town of Sineu is held every week under the eternal gaze of the winged lion

Campos is the centre of the dairy industry, Sant Joan is renowned for its pig farming, and Vilafranca produces melons. The agricultural fair at Inca is the most important farming event on Mallorca, while the livestock market at Sineu is the biggest in the region. Most of the settlements on the plain have no direct access to the sea and suffer from declining populations. Since 1970, the population in towns like Petra has been reduced by half.

Es Plá has been the agricultural heartland of the island since Roman and Moorish occupation. This explains why there is a relatively good road network in the region, with many secondary roads crisscrossing the three main arterial roads – Palma-Alcúdia, Palma-Manacor and Palma-Santanyi. While all of these secondary roads have been tarmacked to deal with the increasing traffic, they have never been diverted from their original position. The majority of them follow the same tracks laid down in medieval times – some even follow the original roads laid out by the Romans.

ALGAIDA

This quiet town (pop. 3100) on the Palma-Manacor road has retained the name given to it by the Arabs – *al-gaida* means 'the woods'. Nowadays the woods have been replaced by extensive almond orchards and olive groves. During the 1980s the town became a mecca for good Mallorcan cuisine. There is a small weekly market which takes place on Fridays. (C-D4)

SHOPPING

Vidrios Gordiola
Glass-blowing factory (founded 1719) and museum.
Daily (except Sun) 09.00-14.00 and 15.00-19.30 hrs; Ctra. Palma-Manacor, 19 km; Tel. 66 50 46

RESTAURANTS

Cal Dimoni
This used to be the main resting place on the journey between the capital and the east coast. Spacious and very rural. Grill. Literally translated the name means 'the house of the devil'!
Daily (except Wed); Ctra. Palma-Manacor, 21 km; Category 2

Can Mateu
Suckling pig a speciality. Garden, children's play area and pool.
Daily (except Tues); Ctra. Palma-Manacor, 21.7 km; Category 2

Els 4 Vents
The inn of the 'four winds' is a reputed restaurant that serves the best in Mallorcan cuisine.
Daily (except Thurs); Ctra. Palma-Manacor, 21 km (next to Cal Dimoni); Category 2

Hostal d'Algaida
Traditional Mallorcan cuisine. Excellent restaurant.
Daily (except Wed); Ctra. Palma-Manacor (by petrol station); Category 2

SURROUNDING AREA

Ermita de Sa Pau
There's a wonderful view of the monastery on Puig de Randa from the tiny 13th-century church. The smiling Renaissance Madonna, *Mare de Déu de Sa Pau* (Madonna of Peace), which gave the church its name, is now kept in the parish church at Algaida. (D4)
Between Algaida and Llucmajor at Castellitx farm (where the key is kept)

Puig de Randa
★ ☆ The 'table mountain', which rises above the apricot orchards to a height of 542 m, lies between Algaida and Llucmajor. It has three 'shelves', each with its own monastery built into it. You approach from the village of Randa. On the first 'shelf', 3 km from the village, is the Santuario de Nuestra Señora de Gracia, a settlement dating back to the 15th century, now abandoned, built like a swallow's nest in a mountain cave. Another kilometre further up the hill stands the Santuari de Sant Honorat which dates back to the 14th century. It is still in use and is therefore not open to visitors. The view from the courtyard is wonderful, however. The Santuari de la Mare de Déu de Cura, Ramón Llull's first mission station, stands on the highest 'shelf', a further 2 km up the mountain. There is overnight accommodation here for pilgrims

MARCO POLO SELECTION: ES PLÁ DE MALLORCA

1 Puig de Randa
Mountain monasteries between Algaida and Llucmajor (page 84)

2 Museu i Fons artístic de Porreres
Contemporary art museum in Porreres (page 87)

3 Cattle market in Sineu
Experience the animated livestock market (page 88)

4 Ermita de Bonany
Great view over the plain, Es Plá de Mallorca, from the settlement above Petra (page 87)

5 Cala Pí
Beautiful, narrow bay at Marina de Llucmajor. Swim in crystal clear waters in a spectacular fjord-like inlet (page 87)

as well as a restaurant. The view from here is magnificent. (D4)
Daily 10.00-19.00 hrs; Tel. 66 09 94

CAMPOS

This lively rural town (pop. 6400) is the market town for the south-eastern agricultural region. The neighbouring towns are all about 14 km away – a day's journey for a farmer who is going to the market with his donkey-drawn cart. There are agricultural fairs in May and October. (D5)

SIGHTS

Santo Cristo de la Paciencia
The painting of Christ in the front right-side chapel of the church of San Julián is by Murillo (c. 1640). The key is kept in the presbytery opposite.

SHOPPING

The two weekly markets on Thursday and Saturday are a good place to find ceramic goods. Try the almond cake in the Pastelería Pomar on the main street.

COSTITX

This little village (pop. 800) is one of the smallest communities on the island. The villagers are mostly farmers and their main crops are almonds, figs and cereals. There is a cottage industry

The monastery of Nuestra Señora de Gracia

that produces artificial roses, crucifixes and Madonnas. (D3)

SIGHTS

Casa de la Fauna Ibero-Balear

The natural history museum has some 3500 stuffed animals and birds on display, reflecting the vast number of different species to be found on the Balearics and Spanish mainland.

Daily (except Sat), 09.00-13.00 and 15.00-19.00 hrs; Sun - mornings only

LLUCMAJOR

Llucmajor (pop. 19 500) is the fourth largest town on the island and around 10% of the island comes under its administrative control. The main industries in the town itself include shoemaking (for Charles Jourdan among others), ceramics and liqueurs. Almonds, apricots and cereal crops are the major produce cultivated on the farmland surrounding the town. Tourism is also important to the local economy. The cliff-edged coastline of Marina de Llucmajor stretches for more than 30 km from S'Arenal on the Playa de Palma to Sa Ràpita, where the sand-dune coast of Es Trenc begins. There are few built-up areas on this southern coast, but where they do exist they tend to be quite extensive, as you will see in Cala Pí and Vallgornera. (C-D5)

SIGHTS

Monument to the Dying King

King Jaime III of Mallorca and his army were defeated by the forces of Pedros IV of Aragón before the gates of the town in 1349. The Monument to the Shoemaker, erected by the town council in honour of its most productive and valued craftsmen, stands right next to the market place.

SHOPPING

Weekly market takes place on Fridays. (No shoes - they're all for the export market!)

HOTELS

Son Sama Country Hotel

Open all year; Ctra. Llucmajor-Porreres; Category 3; Tel. 83 15 83

RESTAURANTS

Can Tiá Taleca

Mallorcan cuisine.
Daily (except Wed); C/. Campos s/n; Category 2; Tel. 66 02 79

Miquel

Seafood restaurant on coast above the fjord-like Cala Pí. Terrace.
Daily in summer, in winter daily (except Mon); Torre Cala Pí s/n; Category 2; Tel. 66 13 09

SPORT

Club Náutico Sa Ràpita

Well-equipped yachting marina with 490 berths. Restaurants. Fuel. Maximum length 20 m.
Tel. 64 04 13

SURROUNDING AREA

Capicorp Vell

Well-preserved and partly reconstructed *talayot* settlement, 12 km south of Llucmajor, with defensive and domestic buildings made of megaliths. Bar. (C5)

Daily (except Thurs), 10.00-18.00 hrs; Entrance 250 ptas

Cala Pí

★ A fjord-like inlet, 3 km long, which opens out into a sandy bay some 20 m wide. Steps have been cut into the cliffs. There is a great view of the island of Cabrera from the medieval watchtower above the beach. (C5)

PETRA

This small town (pop. 2700), founded after the Christian Reconquest, claims to be the spiritual ancestor of San Francisco. The Californian city grew out of a mission set up by the Franciscan friar, Junípero Serra, who was born here (see p.18). It's best to park on the edge of town. (E 3-4)

SIGHTS

Museo del Padre Serra

The museum is dedicated to the memory of Junípero Serra. It displays a diverse collection of letters, drawings, maps and other memorabilia.
Daily; C/. Barracar corner of C/. Fray Junípero Serra (key held at No. 6); Entrance 250 ptas

SHOPPING

Try some *bunyols*, delicious pastries hot from the oven, available from every bakery.

RESTAURANTS

Marina

Bar-cum-restaurant with good, basic Mallorcan cuisine.
Daily (except Mon); C/. Marina 5; Category 3

SURROUNDING AREA

Ermita de Bonany

★ ◁▷ The Bon Any, or 'good year', was 1600 when the rains came after many years of drought. Thanks were given to the Virgin Mary and a temple was erected on the hill. This led to the foundation of a monastery. The present church dates from 1920. There is a splendid view of the Es Plá plain from here. (D4)
Daily 09.00 hrs to sunset; 5 km uphill from Petra; Plaza de la Cruz

PORRERES

This market town (pop. 4500) depends largely on the cultivation of apricots and its vineyards for its income. (D4)

SIGHTS

Nuestra Señora de la Consolación

This church is a magnificent 17th-century building with a square bell tower and a large stained glass window. The sacristy holds the church treasure. The key is kept in the presbytery.

Museu i Fons artístic de Porreres

★ This excellent small museum for contemporary painting and sculpture is located in the town hall. There are about 200 exhibits including two works by Dalí.
Daily (except Sun), during office hours

SURROUNDING AREA

Santuario de Montesión

The monastery of the 'Madonna of Mount Sion' is about 3 km from Porreres. The view from the terrace encompasses Manacor, Campos, Santanyi and Felanitx with the Santuari de San Salvador and the Castell de Santueri. The monastery is now abandoned and there is no access to the monastery church. (D4)

SANT JOAN

Pig farming and sausage-making are the main activities of this village (pop. 1800) along with some cultivation of almonds, fruit and oats. In the 13th century, a miracle is said to have taken place in the hills above Sant Joan. An Arab slave came across a burning bush. In the middle of this bush, unharmed by the flames, was a statue of the Madonna. The slave took the statue with him and built a secret shrine to the Virgin. The Ermita de la Consolació was later built on that very spot. (D4)

SIGHTS

Ermita de la Consolació
This small, stylishly restored church with courtyard and terrace sits amid a multitude of flowers. There are some lovely tiles depicting the stations of the cross. The key is kept in the presbytery of Sant Joan Batista.
Daily 09.00 hrs until sunset

Church of Sant Joan Batista
This church boasts a splendid interior with its roof panelling and alabaster pulpit. A stained glass window portrays the story of the burning bush.

SINEU

This little country town (pop. 2600), which is 30 km east of Palma, is the geographical centre of the island and its history can be traced back some 2000 years. There is a winged lion that stands by the flight of steps leading up to the medieval church of Nuestra Señora de los Ángeles. It is the emblem of St Mark, the patron saint of Sineu. ★ The weekly market (which is principally a cattle market), held every Wednesday on the Plaça d'Espanya around the church, is one of the main attractions. You can get food at very reasonable prices here. (D3)

SIGHTS

Nuestra Señora de los Ángeles
The parish church has a wonderful Gothic dome and a magnificent interior housing the church treasure.
Open Wed

Casa Consistorial
The town hall has a lovely arcade within its courtyard at the centre of which stands a magnificent marble well.
Open during office hours

Centre d'Art S'Estació
This art gallery in the old railway station puts on frequent exhibitions of contemporary art.
Daily (except Mon) 11.00-13.00 and 17.00-19.00 hrs; Tel. 52 07 50

SHOPPING

Weekly market on Wednesdays. Modern art in the art gallery in the old station.

RESTAURANTS

Celler Sa Font
Excellent Mallorcan cuisine.
On Church Square; Category 3

Practical information

Important addresses and other useful information

BANKS AND MONEY

Banks in Mallorca are open only in the morning, usually from 9.00 to 14.30 hrs, Monday to Friday and until 13.00 hrs on Saturday. These times can vary from place to place, but do note that in summer banks close an hour earlier. If you've missed the bank, you'll find *bureaux de change* that stay open all day in all the main resorts. Using a *bureau de change* that isn't authorized by the banks, however, can be expensive. You can change money in most hotels, but again, the exchange rate they offer is never as favourable as at the bank. You get the best rate of exchange with traveller's cheques and Eurocheques (maximum single transaction is currently 25 000 ptas). Most major credit cards are widely accepted and restaurants and shops usually display signs showing which ones they take.

CAR HIRE

There are about 60 car hire firms on the island and their prices are as varied as the vehicles in their fleet. The price lists they issue can sometimes be quite confusing. Some don't include VAT or car insurance, so it's a good idea to double check what's included in the price before you sign on the dotted line. Ask for a small, easily manoeuvrable vehicle and don't forget to take out fully comprehensive insurance. Traffic regulations are the same as in mainland Europe and the speed limit on the motorway (*autopista*) is 120 km/h, and 90 km/h on A roads. Seatbelts must be worn at all times and it is compulsory for motorcyclists to wear crash helmets. Maximum level of alcohol in the blood is 80 ml. The average cost for a small hire car is around 7000 ptas. per day.

CLIMATE

The Balearics enjoy a temperate climate, thanks to their location, though there are marked differences between the islands. Mallorca has a Mediterranean climate – hot, dry summers and mild, wet and generally frost-free winters. The end of July sees the highest temperatures with a daytime average of 30°C. The temperature drops to an average of 14°C in early January. Night-time temperatures range from 6°C in winter to 20°C in summer. Average sea temperatures rise from 13°C in February to 24-26°C in mid-summer. Average hours of sunshine range from five hours in winter to 11 hours in summer. The wettest months are October, September, November and March respectively. Continual rain is the exception rather than the rule, although some storms can be quite severe.

Tourists who wander about Palma in their scanty beachwear will find themselves subject to mockery by the locals. As for men who parade around without their shirts on, they are scathingly referred to as *descamisados,* 'the shirtless ones'. If you go into some bars and restaurants with just your shorts or your bathing costume on, you'll find that you might not get served or if you do, it'll be with great reluctance.

Apart from in the height of summer, the temperature can drop quite noticeably during the evening and it can get quite chilly so it's worth taking a light pullover or cardigan with you when you go out at night.

CONSULATES & EMBASSIES

U.K

Plaza Mayor 3a
Palma
Tel. 71 24 45 and 71 60 48

U.S.A.

Jaime III 26
Palma
Tel.72 26 60

EIRE

Sant Miquel 68
Palma
Tel. 71 92 44

Canada

Edificio Goya
Calle Nunez de Bilbao 35
28001 Madrid
Tel. 431 43 00

You can contact the above addresses for help in emergencies and replacement of travel documents if necessary.

EMERGENCIES

Police (theft and burglary):
Policía Nacional; Tel. 091
Police (traffic accidents):
Policía Municipal; Tel. 092
Guardia Civil; Tel. 062
Medical Emergencies:
Emergency Doctor (24 hrs):
Urgencias Médicas; Tel. 72 22 22
Ambulance: *Tel. 061*
In the resorts there are *Centros Médicos*, with English-speaking personnel.
The Red Cross operates a number of stations on many beaches to provide first aid.
The state-run hospital in Palma is: *Clínica Son Dureta, Tel. 28 91 00*

INFORMATION

Consell de Mallorca
at the airport (Arrivals)

Gobern Balear Tourist Office
Jaime III 10, Palma

Fomento del Turismo de Mallorca
Constitución 1, 1st floor, Palma
Other tourist offices usually operate on a seasonal basis in the major resorts.

NEWSPAPERS, RADIO & TV

You'll find most major European national newspapers in the big resorts and one or two American newspapers and news magazines (usually the *Wall Street Journal*, *Herald Tribune*, *Time* and *Newsweek*). The BBC World Service and The Voice of America are usually quite easy to pick up and there is a radio station based in Palma that broadcasts in English round the clock. Many of the bigger hotels now have satellite TV, which means you can get English-speaking channels.

PARKING

Finding somewhere to park in Palma is a nightmare. In the city centre they have set up a parking control system called ORA *(Ordenación Regulación Aparcamiento)* – which allows limited parking on payment of a fee. You can obtain parking permits in tobacconists (*estancos*). 30 minutes costs 50 ptas., 60 minutes is 75 ptas., 90 minutes, 90 ptas. You fill in your arrival time (month, day, hour, minute) in the appropriate boxes, and the maximum time you can stay in one place is 90 minutes. ORA is in force at all times between 09.30-13.30 hrs and 17.00-20.00 hrs, except for Saturday afternoons and all day Sunday. There is a 70-strong team of traffic wardens who keep a watchful eye on the ORA areas – there's no way you can avoid them. Outside the hours when ORA is in operation, it's almost impossible to find a parking space anyway, so it might be a better idea to use one of the multi-storey car parks. The first hour costs between 100-150 ptas. and 80-100 ptas. for every hour or part of an hour thereafter.

POST AND TELEPHONE

Stamps can be bought at post offices or from tobacconists. It costs 60 ptas. to post a letter or postcard within the EU. The service can be slow and your mail can often take more than a week to reach its destination.

If you use the telephone in your hotel, you could be in for a shock on receiving the bill. It's much more expensive than using a public payphone. When making a call abroad, you need to dial 07 to get an international line. Wait for the dialling tone, then punch in the appropriate country code – 44 for the UK, 1 for the USA and Canada, 353 for Ireland, 61 for Australia and 64 for New Zealand. Cheap rate is from 22.00 to 08.00 hrs.

PUBLIC TRANSPORT

Bus services in Palma itself are good and there is an efficient network connecting the capital to most places on the island. For example, there is a bus every 15 minutes from the centre of Palma down to Playa de Palma. There is a train service which runs five times a day between Palma and Sóller and the journey takes only 50 minutes. But the highlight of the public transport system has to be the single-gauge railway linking Palma and Sóller. It's a fun ride through spectacular scenery and good value for money. You can catch a tram from Sóller to Port de Sóller. There is also a rail link between the capital and Inca.

Journeys within Palma are metred, those outside the capital are calculated on mileage. The prices are regulated by the individual local authorities and each driver must produce a list of these prices on demand.

Taxi-Radio, Palma; Tel. 75 54 40
Taxis Palma Radio; Tel. 40 14 14

The taxi fares for the journey from the airport to the various resorts are listed in the airport arrivals hall. There is an excess charge of 150 ptas. payable for each piece of luggage.

In restaurants, service is usually included in the bill, but it is customary to add between 5 and 10% as a tip. Waiters and chambermaids in hotels can expect to receive between 500 and 1000 ptas., depending on the length of your stay. With taxis, it is usual to round up the fare to the nearest 100 ptas.

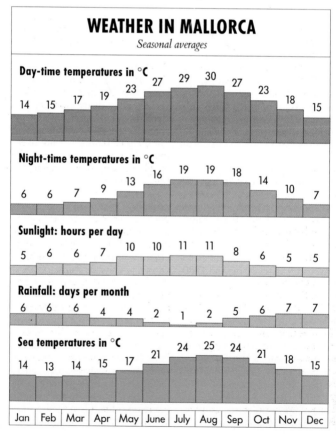

WEATHER IN MALLORCA
Seasonal averages

Day-time temperatures in °C

Jan	Feb	Mar	Apr	May	June	July	Aug	Sep	Oct	Nov	Dec
14	15	17	19	23	27	29	30	27	23	18	15

Night-time temperatures in °C

Jan	Feb	Mar	Apr	May	June	July	Aug	Sep	Oct	Nov	Dec
6	6	7	9	13	16	19	19	18	14	10	7

Sunlight: hours per day

Jan	Feb	Mar	Apr	May	June	July	Aug	Sep	Oct	Nov	Dec
5	6	6	7	10	10	11	11	8	6	5	5

Rainfall: days per month

Jan	Feb	Mar	Apr	May	June	July	Aug	Sep	Oct	Nov	Dec
6	6	6	4	4	2	1	2	5	6	7	7

Sea temperatures in °C

Jan	Feb	Mar	Apr	May	June	July	Aug	Sep	Oct	Nov	Dec
14	13	14	15	17	21	24	25	24	21	18	15

Do's and Don'ts

*How to avoid some of the traps and pitfalls
the unwary traveller may face*

Beach Snacks

They say you only get what you pay for! Well, that's true as a general rule, but if you decide to eat from one of the many beach stalls you'll probably find that this is the exception to the rule. The prices will certainly be in the first-class category, but more often than not, the food is of very poor quality.

Driving

If you do decide to hire a car to drive along the coast, remember that these steep mountainous roads can be treacherous. They are full of hairpin bends and there are few protective barriers to spoil the view!

Fakes and Forgers

Pablo Picasso, Salvador Dalí, Joan Miró – these three Spanish Masters were extraordinarily prolific. Their forgers are even more so. Miró seems to be the most popular one to copy and there are hundreds and hundreds of 'genuine' Mirós on Mallorca. There are few galleries today who would be lucky enough to have a genuine Miró up for sale, but if you want one of the fakes (and some of them are quite good!) make sure you negotiate a fair price.

Flower Girls

You are strolling along minding your own business and a nice young girl gives you a carnation – welcome to Mallorca! What a nice gesture! But if you take the flower, you have to hand over more than just a thank you – it could be the most expensive flower you'll ever buy.

Gambling

Trile is a card game that is played in the resorts, on the streets and at the markets. It's a simple guessing game and is played on an old barrel or upturned box. The players standing around the dealer, the *trilero,* always win. Everyone's in a good mood and, in a spirit of hospitality, the passing tourist is invited to try his luck. The stakes vary between 500 and 5000 ptas. Funnily enough, the stranger never seems to have Lady Luck on his side. This is no quaint custom that helps you get to know the locals – *trile* is just a scam run by card sharps.

Mystery Tours

Strangely enough, these mystery tours always seem to end up at some place where someone is trying to sell you something. The organizers are experts in psychology and use the outward trip to get your sympathy for the impoverished conditions some of the 'craftsmen' have to work and live in. You'll end up feeling almost morally bound to buy something, if only to cover the organizers' costs. Remember, if you do find yourself on one of these tours, you are not obliged to buy anything. So just sit back and enjoy the views. You don't have to worry about being unscrupulous. The organizers certainly don't.

Pedlars

These street sellers, mainly from North and West Africa, can be quite persistent in trying to sell you their wares. You will come across them on the beaches, promenades and beach-side bars with their trays laden with watches, sunglasses, jewellery, cassettes, African masks and trinkets galore. They've become an integral part of the tourist landscape and although it's illegal for them to trade, the police usually turn a blind eye to their activities. But remember that all that glistens isn't necessarily gold and that if you do decide to buy that 'Vuitton' bag or 'Rolex', just enjoy the fact that you've had a bit of fun bargaining for fake goods!

Trips

The first organized day trips on Mallorca were run by the *Fomento de Turismo*, the Mallorcan Tourist Board, way back in 1905. The format (and the routes) haven't changed all that much since then. There are always plenty of commercial stops at souvenir shops, leather factories and distilleries, where the tourist is welcomed with open arms. If you do decide to take one of these trips, then it's a good idea to find out exactly how much time you will spend shopping and how much sightseeing you'll actually get done.

Table Manners

Don't be tempted to sit at a table that has already got someone sitting at it. This goes for bars and street cafés as much as for restaurants. Spaniards consider the question 'Is anyone sitting here?' to be the worst form of bad manners! Just about as bad is going into a restaurant and not waiting to be shown to your table. If you do that then the chances are you'll have to put up with poor service or even no service at all.

VAT

To some hoteliers, restaurateurs and shopkeepers VAT (IVA) is just something to play with. Some include it in the price, others don't. It's worth checking the menu to see whether VAT at 15% is included or extra. It is not compulsory to include VAT in prices quoted, but you should be aware of the possible hidden cost and that the bargain you thought was such good value might not be so cheap after all!

Water

It's best to drink bottled water as a rule. Water from the tap is not harmful, but doesn't taste that good. Carbonated water is called *agua con gas* and still water is *agua sin gas*.

INDEX

This index lists all the main sights and places mentioned in this guide

What do you get for your money?

Given the frequent fluctuations in the exchange rate it's impossible to say exactly what your money's worth in pesetas. You won't go far wrong though, if you reckon on getting about 200 ptas. to the pound or 125 ptas. to the dollar. Some typical prices. A *café solo* (espresso) costs about 75-150 ptas., a croissant about the same. A packet of Spanish cigarettes costs between 100-150 ptas. Cinema tickets are priced from 500 ptas. upwards. A bottle of average quality Spanish wine costs between 500-800 ptas. in the supermarket – expect to pay double or even triple the price in a restaurant. 450 ptas. should get you a Campari and soda in a street café – a bottle of the same will cost you about 1200 ptas. in the supermarket. A bottle of Spanish brandy (*coñac*) can cost about 1000 ptas. and a litre of mineral water around 150 ptas. Entrance fees for museums range between 200-500 ptas. and water parks can charge around 1500 ptas. for adults, and half the adult price for children. An evening at a restaurant with a cabaret can cost in the region of 6000 ptas., meal included. A hired car (eg Ford Fiesta) with fully comprehensive insurance can cost 5000 ptas. per day, fuel not included.

The conversion chart below gives you a rough idea of what your money's worth.

£	Ptas	$
0.60	125	1.00
1.00	200	1.60
2.00	400	3.20
2.50	500	4.00
3.75	750	6.00
5.00	1000	8.00
10.00	2000	16.00
15.00	3000	24.00
20.00	4000	32.00
25.00	5000	40.00
50.00	10000	80.00
75.00	15000	120.00
100.00	20000	160.00
150.00	30000	240.00
200.00	40000	320.00
250.00	50000	400.00
500.00	100 000	800.00